TRAIL ORIENTEERING

an outdoor activity for people with disabilities

ANNE BRAGGINS

Produced with support from the
British Orienteering Federation and the Sports Council

Published 1993 by:

HARVEYS
12-16 Main Street, Doune, Perthshire FK16 6BJ.
Tel: 0786 841202. Fax: 0786 841098.

ISBN 1 85137 0900.

Typesetting, design and layout by Harveys, Doune.

Printed by Alna Press, Broxburn.

Acknowledgements

Funds for this project have been secured by Barwell Sports Management from Marks & Spencer plc and John Rothschild Holdings Charitable Trust, and are made available through the charity PHAB (Physically Handicapped - Able Bodied). The steering committee consists of representatives of the British Orienteering Federation, Barwell Consulting, PHAB, British Sports Association for the Disabled and the Sports Council.

To all who have supplied material for, and been good enough to comment on the draft, our thanks.
Anne Braggins.

Cover photograph: Camilo de Mendonca.

Cartoons by Guthrie Hutton.

Exercise illustrations by Ian Whalley.

Maps and diagrams are reproduced with permission from London Orienteering Klubb, King Edward Foundation, Harvey Maps. Copyright reserved.

Adapted extracts from *Orienteering in the National Curriculum* with permission of the publishers. Copyright reserved.

Contents

Foreward

One of the most exciting developments for disabled people in the last 15 years or so has been the opening up of many recreational activities which hitherto had barely seemed possible. Despite a huge increase in both standards and participation that has occurred in the more traditional sports, participation in outdoor activities has expanded even faster.

Much of this development began within the "disabled" community itself, with relatively little input from the relevant national governing body. But as interest in these activities increased, the need for governing body involvement became more evident. This book is an impressive example of how seriously one governing body, the British Orienteering Federation, takes its responsibilities for opening up the sport of orienteering to everyone who wants to have a go.

It is addressed to all those who might become involved with someone with a disability who fancies trying orienteering, - clubs, schools, relatives and friends - as well as the individual with a disability him/herself. It is detailed enough for the absolute beginner to discover both the what and the how, and at the same time shows the long standing enthusiast how they can extend their involvement in the sport by helping to access it for others. Orienteering is called the "Thought Sport"; this book deserves a wide readership, and BOF are to be congratulated for their imaginative step in getting it into production.

Tim Marshall, MBE
Member of the Sports Council

Chapter 1 A New Challenge

Sport is for all. The involvement may be a sedentary affair involving the pressing of a few buttons in front of a television set in your own home, or something a bit closer as a spectator at a match or other sporting event. Vast numbers participate at a low level in sport because they enjoy some physical activity and the companionship of other like-minded people. The elite, those at the top of their chosen sport devote all their free time to achieving selection for a national World Cup team or the Olympics. The skill, technique and determination are evident for all to see as these events are beamed across the world. The joy and pride of being there applies equally to those of a sporting community known as the 'disabled athletes' at the Paralympics when the competitors not only have to be the best at their chosen sport but have overcome some physical impairment or a learning difficulty on the way to the top.

The opportunities open to people previously regarded as being barred from active sport have increased tremendously in recent years, and rightly so. Sports organising bodies have shown great ingenuity, working in co-operation with disabled people and those involved with them, in overcoming difficulties, adapting some events and inventing others and modifying techniques and equipment. The simple premise from which it all starts is 'yes I can' rather than 'no I can't'.

This book starts from the same premise, and it speaks for another sporting community - that of orienteering. It is intended for disabled people and anyone who might bring them and orienteeering together. Throughout we will use the term 'escorts' to refer to people who help a disabled person in any way during their normal life, be they parents, other family members, friends, teachers, care assistants or the many others that could be listed. There are also those involved in providing facilities, or those organising activities for disabled people, at school, or maybe through a sports or social club.

Photo: Kenth Karlsson

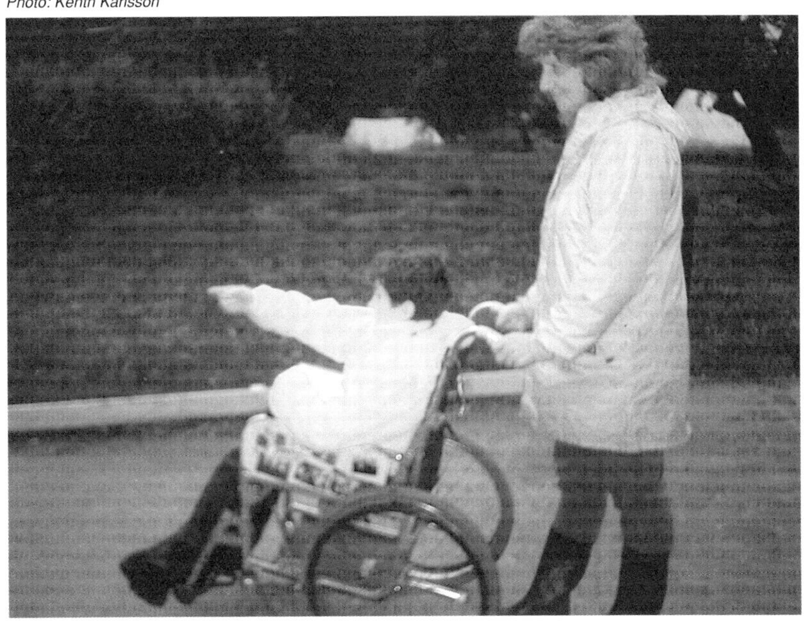

Orienteering is (with occasional exceptions) an individual rather than a team sport. It is however a very social recreation, not least because, certainly in Britain, its community is still relatively small. The sport's many different classes mean that once you begin to enter competitions, you also begin to recognise faces turning up regularly in your own class. Then you can put names to the faces, make contact, and establish friendships.

In recent years orienteers have begun to realise that the sport they enjoy so much can be adapted to allow disabled people to enjoy it too, and moves to expand the orienteering community to take in disabled groups are starting in many places. The idea of people in wheelchairs, or with learning difficulties, successfully attempting a sport the essence of which is fast travel over difficult country might appear absurd, but it is now accepted that there is no need to approach it in that way. Orienteering can be untimed, and still be a thoroughly enjoyable activity and great fun. For true competition, a form of the sport called Trail Orienteering has been developed which is designed for people whose mobility is less than that of other orienteers.

We believe that Trail O, although a physical activity, is rare among sports in that the physical capacity of the competitor is irrelevant to the level achieved in competition. It is therefore open to those in all impaired mobility groups with participants competing on equal terms. Visual impairment and mental ability may cause some limitations.

Forms of orienteering have also been devised that can be used in the indoor environment by many disabled people. These introduce them very gently to the sport as a fun activity with absolutely no competitive pressure, though it can be surprising how quickly a demand for competition can develop. It is something different, something disabled people, or their escorts may not have thought of as a possibility. This book sets out to show that the possibility does indeed exist and that many disabled people can enjoy orienteering as a new recreational activity, a countryside outing with something extra. The established orienteering community is committed to doing all it can to help this expansion take place, and to welcome as many people as possible to a world in which the horizons are almost limitless.

In this book we start with orienteering at the grass roots. After explaining what it is and giving some guidance on how to introduce disabled people to the concept of orienteering, the book then shows how the new orienteer can begin to reach out as knowledge and confidence grow to expand the horizons, very gently at first into local familiar areas such as parks, and then, if the desire is there, to compete alongside other orienteers at mainstream events. For a few, the route will lead on to harder and harder competition, to championships, and perhaps events in other countries.

Orienteering has a well-established world structure, recognised by the International Olympic Committee (though it is not yet part of the Games programme). Whether the sport is experienced at the very simplest level of fun and recreation, or enjoyed in top competition, is entirely up to the individual. We invite people with disabilities to join us in the orienteering community and hope that after reading this book, many will seek out and enjoy this new challenge.

Chapter 2 What Is Orienteering?

In understanding what orienteering is, it will be necessary to introduce a modest amount of terminology as would be true of any sport. The basic orienteering terms and orienteering organisation - what we have called the 'mechanics of orienteering' - are explained in chapter 4. This chapter aims to introduce the concept of orienteering both as a non-competitive, fun activity and as a competitive sport, and to do that we must start with the word itself.

The dictionary defines orienteering as 'the sport of making one's way quickly across difficult country with the help of map and compass'. This is not especially helpful for disabled competitors because they don't need to go quickly, and the country need in no way be difficult. However the reference to map and compass is entirely apt.

Going back to the root, 'orient', helps a little more. One meaning is simply 'the east', but it also means, again according to the dictionary, 'to place in a definite relation to the points of the compass or other fixed or known directions'. That too can be greatly simplified to mean that you know where you are in relation to your surroundings, you know where you want to go next, and you know in what direction you should travel to get there.

At a control

Drawing: Guthrie Hutton

Now we are getting closer to a definition of the sport of orienteering though purists would insist that any definition should include an element of route choice. Orienteering is therefore a navigational sport in which the competitors, or 'orienteers' use a detailed map and with the aid of a compass, locate in the landscape a number of pre-identified checkpoints in a specified order. These are usually small features either natural or man-made.

As each point is reached, competitors mark a card as proof of their visit. In most cases the person who completes the course in the fastest time is the winner. This time element has been removed from Trail O to eliminate any advantage that could be gained by those using, for instance, superior wheelchairs. This allows all to compete together.

Orienteering started in the extensive forests of Scandinavia in the 1920s. In its earliest days it was used for military training, but it was very quickly realised that here was a splendid new sport for all, that made use of an almost limitless natural resource. Scandinavian forests grow on highly detailed, glaciated terrain with a proliferation of small detail. The ground dips, rises and bends in an endless series of little knolls and valleys, and in the Scandinavian countries orienteering has been very much based on this 'contour detail'.

A contour line is an imaginary line which joins all points of the same altitude.

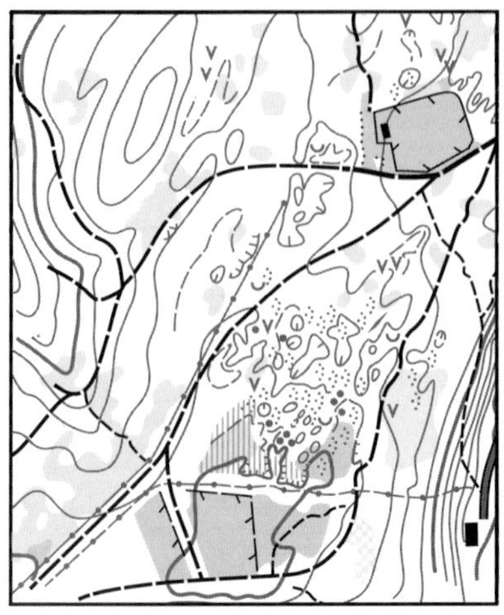

Above: map of complex forest terrain (1:10,000)

Below: map of simpler (parkland) terrain (1:5,000)

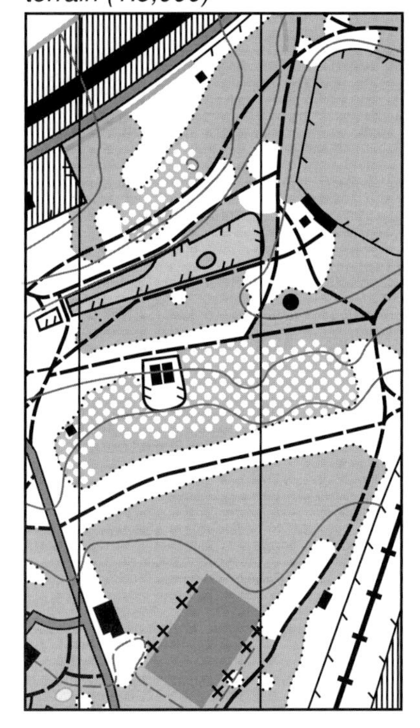

It was soon found that the basic government maps did not give sufficient detail, so orienteers, who are resourceful folk, simply set to work to survey and draw their own maps. These maps have developed to the point where they are now almost artforms, so wonderfully detailed are they and so well do they depict the terrain. Orienteering stayed mainly as a Scandinavian sport until about 1960, when other countries began to enjoy it and spread the message.

Orienteering has been well established in Britain since the late 1960's. The sport here is controlled by the British Orienteering Federation (BOF) and events take place, usually at weekends, throughout the year. Britain does not have the extensive forests of Scandinavia, and great ingenuity has been shown in making use of initially unpromising areas of terrain including parks, moorland, stable sand-dunes and urban fringes to provide a strong basis for the sport. The specially drawn large-scale maps depict much more ground detail than normal maps, adding variety and interest to the navigational challenge. The sport is popular with people of all ages.

At one level, orienteering is a highly competitive sport. However, one of the great beauties of orienteering is that it need not be a competitive activity. It can be a non-competitive recreation or simply a fun activity, and in this guise is very popular with children. It can also be popular with people with disabilities, of whatever kind.

In chapters 5 & 6 we show how a simplified form of orienteering can be enjoyed in the home environment, wherever that may be. Although competitive orienteering takes place outdoors you can have a lot of fun devising an indoor course, and following it round using everyday objects as your checkpoints.

However simple the activity becomes, in essence it retains the same structure, presenting a challenge to complete the course by finding all the points in the right order, whether this happens in a hall, playground, park or forest.

It is very much our hope that once introduced to orienteering, disabled people will want to become part of the wider orienteering community. Not the least reason for this is that the mainstream sport naturally takes place in some of our most attractive areas of countryside, places which are in themselves a delight to visit and enjoy.

This, then, is orienteering. It has been encapsulated in a number of amusing slogans over the years. Particularly appropriate is 'the thought sport'. Perhaps it is best simply to think of it, as the next chapter tries to show, as a countryside sport open to everyone.

Chapter 3 A Sport For All

Orienteers throughout the world are well aware of how fortunate they are to take part in their sport. They enjoy the mental and physical challenges of navigating through varied terrain with map and compass, and the opportunity to socialise as well as compete with fellow outdoor enthusiasts. So far, these opportunities have not been fully available to the substantial number of men, women and children who are disabled.

In 1992 the International Orienteering Federation (IOF) set up a working group to help orienteering federations worldwide integrate people with disabilities into mainstream orienteering and share with them the very many happy opportunities the sport provides.

The intention is not to set up special events for disability groups or individuals, although on certain occasions this may occur, but to provide access for competition on specially planned courses that run alongside other courses at mainstream events. The main version on offer will be Trail Orienteering, so called as the competitor remains on the track or trail. It is defined as 'untimed courses where the challenge is mental and achievement is based upon the ability to interpret correctly the map and its relationship to the ground'.

This will allow access for the physically disabled, those temporarily disabled through injury (sprained ankle, broken leg, etc), people with learning difficulties, and others unable to compete in rough terrain.

It is accepted that certain problems may arise when the participants are disabled. For example, many people with disabilities are reliant on special transport, often provided by local authorities or voluntary organisations, and may only be available for daytime activities. Initial experience in Trail Orienteering is likely to be at special schools and centres, or on holiday occasions. However, orienteering clubs may well be able to assist with special events and if requested may put on competitive Trail Orienteering courses at some events on their fixture list. Local authorities and other landowners can provide suitable permanent facilities for Trail Orienteering when considering other provision for those with disabilities.

Photo: Glynn Roberts

Orienteering clubs putting on competitive Trail Orienteering courses will also need to realise that many residential institutions have an early evening meal and therefore cannot attend evening events without severely disrupting their normal schedules. Those attending day centres must return home with the scheduled transport and will only be able to attend orienteering events if the whole group is able to go. However, as with all orienteering converts, such problems will always be overcome, and co-operation with local disability groups can bring mutual benefits. After all, the intention is that Trail O should become a valid activity for all club members, and once incorporated in the fixture pattern, new members will have a lot to offer the club in return.

The nature of competitive Trail O is fully explained in chapter 8, which shows how there is a 'pyramid' of competition reaching from the basic course to an elite one for the very experienced competitor - i.e. from local, informal fun competitions to national championships. Coaching will be available to those who wish it, and some will achieve the glory of representing their country in international competition.

As with orienteering in general there is, however, no compulsion for any person to move up the pyramid. The main consideration is that orienteering should be accepted as a valid activity for disabled people, and that in turn they and their escorts should know a little about orienteering, and its enjoyable recreational dimensions.

Orienteering wishes to be seen as a non-exclusive activity and has made considerable strides in that direction in recent years. A number of regular events now include Trail O courses alongside the mainstream orienteering age or colour-coded courses. The first permanent Trail O course in Britain was opened on Forestry Commission land at Whinlatter in the Lake District in autumn 1992 (see Chapter 7).

The map-reading element of most Trail O courses may mean that they are not suitable for all people with learning difficulties, but orienteering can cater for them too. Many orienteering events provide 'string' courses which are principally aimed at complete beginners and young children. These courses literally follow a string or tape, with checkpoints at regular intervals. There is often a fun element, with cartoon figures at the checkpoints and badges as prizes. Another possibility is to 'run' with a buddy on a colour coded course (see next chapter).

Running with a buddy

Drawing: Guthrie Hutton

Nor is there any question of disabled people being cast out into the orienteering world on their own. Not only are disabled people considered to be part of the orienteering community, but escorts, be they friends, relatives or club members are positively encouraged to accompany the disabled orienteer round the courses. In some cases, such as wheelchair competitors, this will be necessary anyway, but in every case, if it helps, then organisers will encourage it.

For those who <u>are</u> restricted physically, considerable care is taken to ensure that Trail O courses are properly accessible. The course is planned with wheelchairs in mind and whenever possible is tested with a wheelchair beforehand. Lower eye levels are also taken into consideration when looking for specific points in the terrain.

This chapter has largely concentrated on Trail Orienteering as being the main way in which disabled people can enjoy the sport. However, as has already been mentioned, there are many ways in which simple variations of the sport can be provided indoors or in areas such as playgrounds and parks. These variations, already used when introducing schoolchildren to the concept of orienteering, are detailed in chapters 5 and 6. They really do mean that no-one is left out, and they provide a wonderfully simple and enjoyable platform on which to build confidence and enjoyment and from which the great adventure of orienteering in the wider environment can be launched.

Chapter 4 The Mechanics of Orienteering

Like all sports and recreations, orienteering has its own special terms both for techniques employed and for pieces of equipment regularly used while taking part. This chapter takes you, the potential competitor or group activity organiser, through a Trail orienteering event from start to finish, explaining each of the terms as it arises, so that by the end of the chapter, you should know what these terms mean when you come across them in future.

The event we are going to describe is a local one, typical of those staged in many parts of Britain. Pre-event publicity consists of an information sheet like the one shown here.

Typical event information sheet

TRAIL ORIENTEERING

Your chance to experience Trail O - an orienteering discipline where those with disabilities can compete on equal terms with the able-bodied and those recovering from injury, unfit or infirm. The disability is immaterial as there are courses suitable for everyone, unless visual impairment is severe.

Orienteering is a navigational sport and competitors locate specific control sites with the aid of a detailed map. The routes are carefully chosen so that those in wheelchairs can take part with others. There will be people around to explain what you have to do but you should bring an escort to give any physical assistance that may be required.

Date: ***Friday 9th April***

Venue: ***War Memorial Park, Basingstoke***
Attractive town park with a good path system, grassed areas, flower beds and trees, with play and sports fields.

Parking: ***At the Civic Offices car park***
Approached down White Hart Lane, off London Road.

Toilets: ***Will be available in the John Arlott Pavilion****, reached from Crossborough Hill, off London Road, you should visit these before parking.*

Entry Fee: ***£2.00 for adults and £1.00 for juniors*** *(under 21).*

Registration: ***15.00 - 17.00****, at the red tent.*

Courses ***Cream - very easy****. Basic courses suitable for children and novices with no map experience. Similar to white/ yellow colour coded courses at mainstream events.*

Rose - easy*. There will be two control markers at each control site, the competitor has to decide which of the two is shown by the centre of the control circle and punch their control card accordingly.*

Sky - medium*. With three control markers to choose from at each site.*

Further information from:
BOF National Office, Riversdale, Dale Road North, Darley Dale, Matlock, DE4 2JB. Phone 0763 260333.
Organised on behalf of the British Orienteering Federation.

This information sheet gives the date of the event, the organising club with a contact name, address and telephone number, the position of car park and assembly areas, the times between which starts are available, and an outline of the courses, with a brief description of the terrain or type of country being used. This latter might be parkland, moorland, forest, foreshore, or a combination of any of these. The event will also be advertised in the club newsletter and that of the regional orienteering association, and possibly in the local press.

It is appreciated if disabled people, especially groups, contact the organisers in advance to let them know that you would like to come and to discuss special arrangements for parking, toilets etc. These matters are considered in more detail in chapter 6. For the purposes of this chapter, let us assume that you have contacted the organiser and confirmed that there is a suitable course for disabled people, including those in wheelchairs. In Britain a standard colour-coding system is used everywhere for club events, ranging from white, which is the easiest, up to brown or black, the hardest. The Trail-

O equivalents are cream to grey. The cream course may well be the same as the white or yellow one at many events.

You have arrived at the event in good time, parked, and are getting ready to start. The first important place is **registration**. Here you select which course you are going to do. As with all first timers, you are advised to do the easiest course on offer as this gives a chance to concentrate on the map. You may well be offered the chance to a second, more technical, course when you have completed the first one. If time allows, do take advantage of this offer.

TRAIL ORIENTEERING NAME .... COURSE .... CLUB .... START									
21	22	23	24	25	26	27	28	29	30
11	12	13	14	15	16	17	18	19	20
1	2	3	4	5	6	7	8	9	10

Above: control card
Below: control description sheet and the alternative IOF pictorial control descriptions (see Appendix D)

Cream (Novice - N) Course 1.3km

Start		Road
1	N1	Road bend
2	N2	Road/track junction
3	N3	Track/path junction
4	N4	Thicket
5	N5	Bridge
6	N6	Path junction
7	N7	Path junction
8	N8	Path/ditch junction
9	N9	Track/stream crossing
10	N10	Track junction

Navigate to finish

Cream		1.300m				
▷						
1	N1					
2	N2					
3	N3					
4	N4					
5	N5					
6	N6					
7	N7					
8	N8					
9	N9					
10	N10					

You pay your entry fee and are given a **control card** with an allocated start time. Starts on each course are normally at one-minute intervals so that you have space to maneouvre.

The **control card** is illustrated opposite. It has spaces for the competitor's name, club, class or course, start and finish times, and rows of numbered boxes. These boxes are for you to use as you reach each **control point** around the course.

Trail orienteering will use maps pre-printed with your course and will have an attached **control description sheet.** They will not be given to you until you start to prevent you studying the course beforehand.

The **control description sheet** is just that. The description sheet for a cream (novice) course is shown left. It gives the name or class of your course and the control numbers in the order in which they must be visited, the **control code** which will be found associated with the **control marker** when you get there, and the actual description of the feature you are looking for.

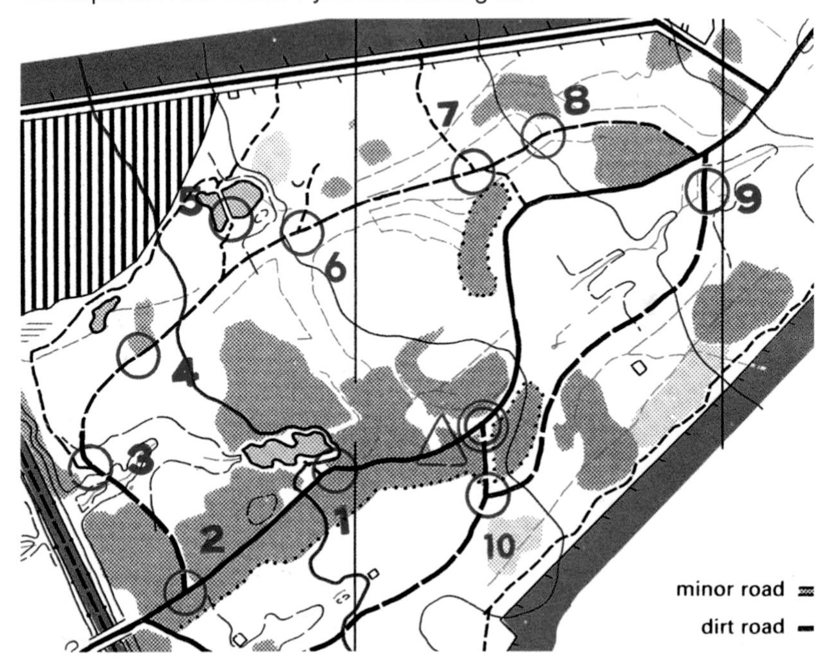

As you will see, all the features are very clear and definite. On cream, white and yellow course controls are usually either on or near paths, to make the navigation as easy as possible. We want everybody starting orienteering and trying simple courses to enjoy the experience and complete the course successfully, leaving them wanting to try again next time there is a local event.

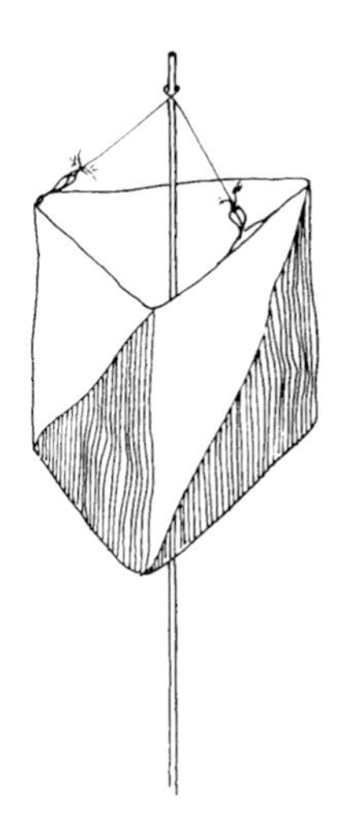

Above: control marker

Below: control punch

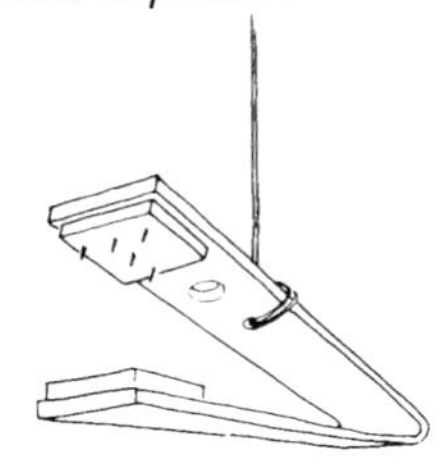

You will be issued with a 'punch' or one or more will be hung from the control marker. This is a V-shaped device with, at the open end of the V, small pins on one side which can be pressed down onto a pad on the other.

When you reach the control marker and have checked by its code that it is the one you are looking for, you punch your control card in the appropriate box with this little pin-punch. You carry on doing this all round the course until, in the case of the course referred to above, you should have ten punchmarks in boxes 1 to 10 on your control card.

Now let's get to the **start**. Assuming that your start time is 11.30, you should aim to be at the start about 11.15 The start procedure usually takes three or four minutes and it is worth having a few minutes in hand just to check that you have everything, and to look at the start area and make sure you understand what is going on.

You will see that people are being assembled by their start time, and you will hear officials calling out the time at one-minute intervals, and a whistle blowing as competitors actually start. Disabled competitors may well have their own start, or a separate 'lane' at the main start, and this will have been made clear to you beforehand. If you are starting at 11.30, you will probably be called up to get into the start lanes at 11.27. At that time the 'pre-start' official will call out '11.30 starts' and your control card will be checked to make sure that you are coming forward at the right time.

You get into line with the others starting at 11.30. At 11.28, the whistle blows and you move forward to the next box or line. At major events, this is when the adrenalin really starts to flow and you begin to feel both nervous and excited, wondering what lies ahead and how well you will do. Even at a club event you can get a tingle of anticipation.

At the Start

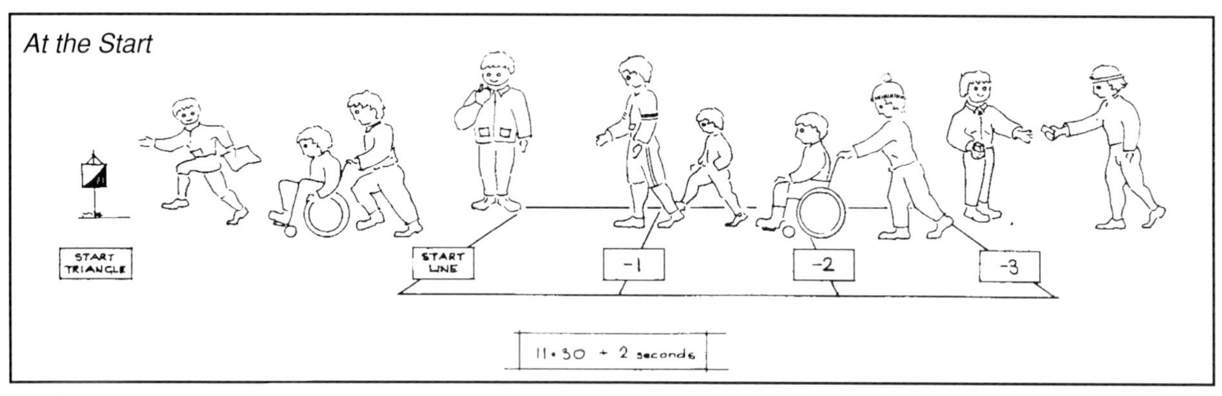

Drawing: Guthrie Hutton

How the course appears on the map

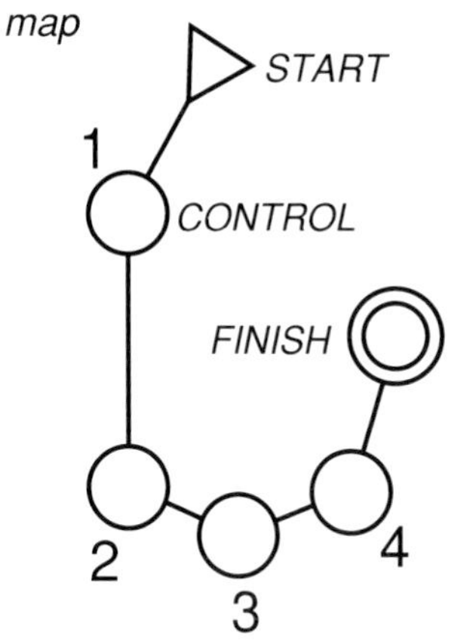

At 11.29 you move onto the start line itself, and now have a minute before you actually start. You will receive the map unit, including the control description sheet with 10 seconds to go.

There is a countdown of 'ten seconds', 'five seconds', the whistle blows and you're off - your orienteering adventure has started! You can now start thinking about the course.

The **start** is shown by a triangle. The **control**s are shown by circles. The feature being used for the control must be exactly in the centre of the circle, so that there is no doubt about it - in very detailed areas with lots of features there could be several boulders, for example, in the circle.

The **finish** is shown by a double circle.

Now we'll go back to the course and your route to the first control. The most important piece of advice at this stage is **ignore everybody else**. It can be very confusing for beginners with people apparently moving in all directions. Just concentrate on your course, your next control and take it at your pace. Go along the road to the bend and look for the red-and-white marker with the code N1 attached. Sure enough, there it is - your first control!

You put your card into the punch, making sure that you are punching in box no 1, press the pins down firmly onto the pad, and that's it - your visit has been recorded.

You have now covered most of the basic mechanics of orienteering. You are using a map, control card and control description sheet, you have been through the registration and start procedures, and you have reached the first control and punched your card. You can relax a bit and really start to enjoy the experience, enjoy the scenery as well as finding the controls.

By continuing along the road you will come to your second control, and from there you turn right, north in this case, up a track towards control number 3.

Examples of line features: path/fence crossing, path/stream crossing

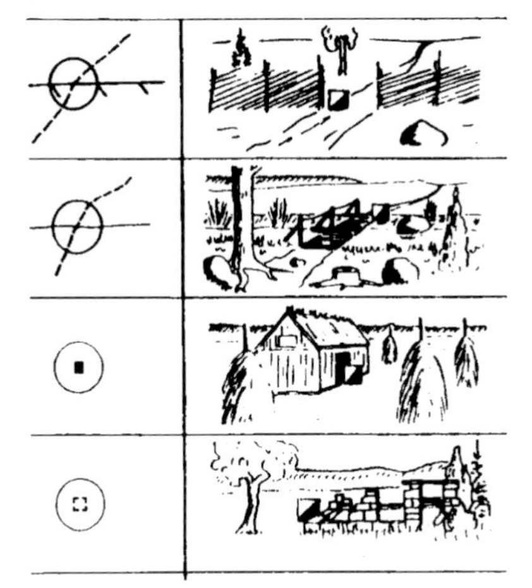

Examples of point features: building, ruin

This is a good time at which to mention the two main types of features used for orienteering controls - **line features** and **point features**. If you think about those terms, you will understand the difference. A line feature is something that runs across the terrain (and thus the map) for some distance, and a path is obviously such a feature. Other line features include streams, walls and fences. A point feature is a definite, individual object or feature in the landscape.

Only very obvious point features are used on novice courses. Most control markers will be on line features, as on this course.
It is often reasonably easy to see the last control on a course as it is probably common to a number of courses and there will be lots of people aiming for it. Once you have reached it and marked your card you only have to navigate to the **finish**.

In a local event such as this one, the finish is often quite close to the assembly area and before long you are back at your transport, meeting others who have been out and comparing notes. There will be a **results display** nearby on which your result is put up once your card has been checked and the correct punch marks verified. You will often find details of future events available here too.

The Results Display

Drawing: Guthrie Hutton

This gives a general outline of what happens at an outdoor orienteering event. Beginners often comment that it gives an outing a purpose. At a higher level in competitive Trail Orienteering, the system at controls is a little different, in order to try to give fair competition based on problem-solving rather than on just recording progress round the course. This is all explained in chapter 8. But that's a few stages ahead for many disabled people starting to try orienteering as a new activity. For their first attempts, it may be better to stay in the home environment, or very close to it, and the next chapter looks at ways in which this can be done.

Chapter 5 Getting Started

Having explained what orienteering is about, it is now time to turn our attention to how the sport can be introduced to disabled people. Many will be able to go straight into competitive Trail Orienteering. They will find the next two chapters provide some background before concentrating on chapter 8, and it is often worth talking to an orienteer and looking at some maps indoors before going to an event. To find an orienteer contact your National Federation, the addresses are given in Appendix B.

Others would not wish to start so quickly, so the introduction for them must begin at a much simpler and more approachable level. This chapter is particularly appropriate for teachers of children and those involved with people who have learning difficulties, or maybe those lacking in self confidence who would be happier initially in home surroundings. It gives a few suggestions to get started, first indoors and then in the school or institution grounds. Many other ideas will be found in the educational books listed in Appendix F.

EQUIPMENT
Tabletop picture maps
Coloured pencils
Model houses, trees and a model car
String
Boards to lean on

OBJECTIVES
- *To reinforce the concept that a map is like a picture*
- *To see how a map can be used to show, and help you follow, a route*
- *To locate positions on a map*
- *To follow directions*
- *To develop understanding of the following terms: PICTURE MAP, SET, ROUTE, SYMBOLS, PLAN, DIRECTIONS*

USING TABLETOP PICTURE MAPS

Preparation

Draw a simple picture map and a plan of a table top model or copy the ones shown on the next page.

Lesson

1. Set up the model to match the map. Give each member of the group a copy of the picture map. The participants should stand or sit

round 3 sides of the model so that they can relate their picture maps to the model. Ask them to set their maps and identify each of the houses and trees.

2. Introduce the model car, which is going on a tour, visiting each of the houses. As the car is directed along its route everyone follows where it goes on their picture maps, continually locating its position. Use the terms 'left' and 'right'.

3. Choose a new starting point. The group members draw in the route the car takes as it goes from house to house. A piece of string along the route on the model will show the correct line. Arrows on the line will show the direction the car is going.

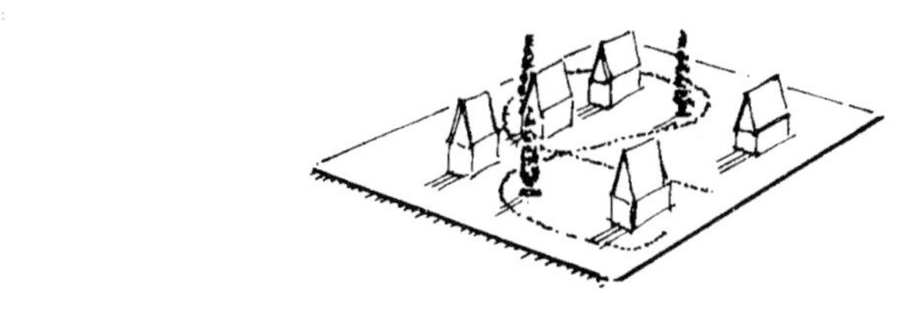

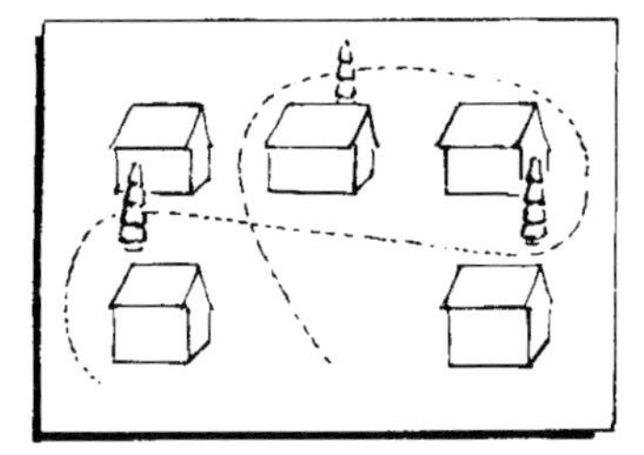

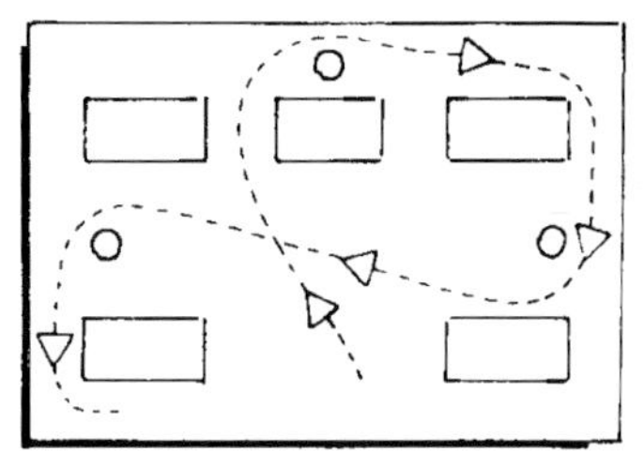

4. Give each member of the group a plan of the model. Compare and match the picture map and the plan with each other and with the model. Identify the symbols showing trees and houses. Set the plan. Locate the start point of the route shown by the string and already drawn on the picture maps. Draw the route on to the plan by looking at the line of the string. Compare it with the line on the picture map.

Summary
Maps are made up of symbols. Symbols are map language. The symbols can be read and seen as pictures of the features they represent. A map can be used to plan and follow a route.

Follow up
Participants can make their own models and then make picture maps or plans of them. Plot in routes using string, and then transfer them on to the map.

The same plans can be used to introduce the cardinal compass points, along with a globe and maps of the world. Use the compass to establish north. Place the model orientated to north. Label the model and the plans, marking north, south, east and west. Describe the location and direction of the features. Describe the routes according to directions taken.

EQUIPMENT
Treasure island features, e.g. lake (water basin), river (blue rope or cord), house (box), trees (skittles or cones), field (outline with canes or rope), tracks (chalked lines) + paper, clipboards, crayons (blue, green, black, brown, red)

A TREASURE ISLAND

Preparation
Collect equipment. Decide which area to use: young children need to be able to overlook the whole area; older people can use a larger area with bigger features. With children read a story about an island.

OBJECTIVES
- *To establish the meaning of the word "set" and follow up the use of shapes and symbols*
- *To extract information and add it to pictorial maps*
- *To make representation of imaginary places*
- *To follow a route and locate position*
- *To give instructions for movement along a route*
- *To develop understanding of the following terms: MAP, SET, ROUTE*

Exercise

1. If appropriate give out paper, boards, crayons. Seat participants round the area to be used for the island.

2. Using chalk or rope, mark out the coastline of the island in a simple shape. As you add features on the island, the participants or assistants draw them on the paper. A mixture of pictures and symbols is quite acceptable for this map.

3. Place large features first: the lake (basin of water) and the river (blue cord) leading to it; the box as the house; the cones (or pot plants) can represent trees; a chair can be a lookout tower. A field can be used to fill in the gaps.

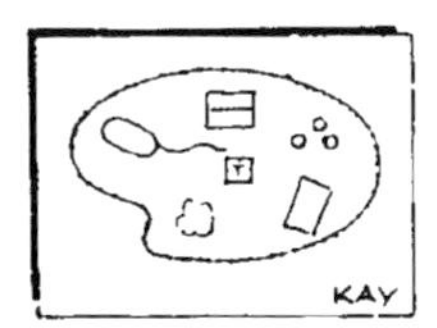

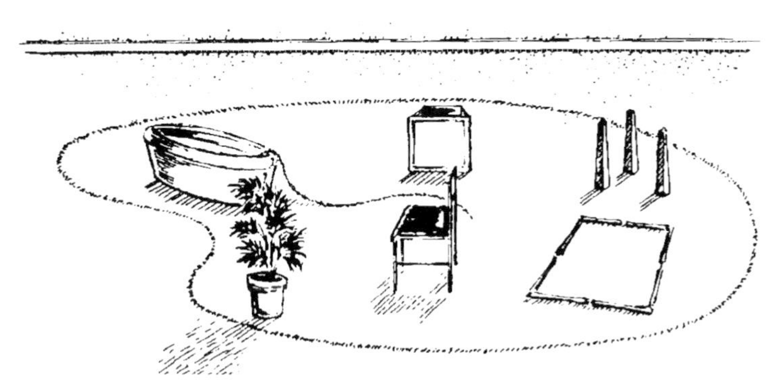

4. **Story line**

Following a shipwreck a box of treasure is buried. Before being rescued the mariners make a map of the island so that the treasure can be found later. The group are the ship-wrecked mariners.

Ask where they want to bury their treasure. Mark the place with a 'T'.

Now years later you return to dig up your treasure and land on the island at the point where you are sitting. Have it marked on the map with an arrow.

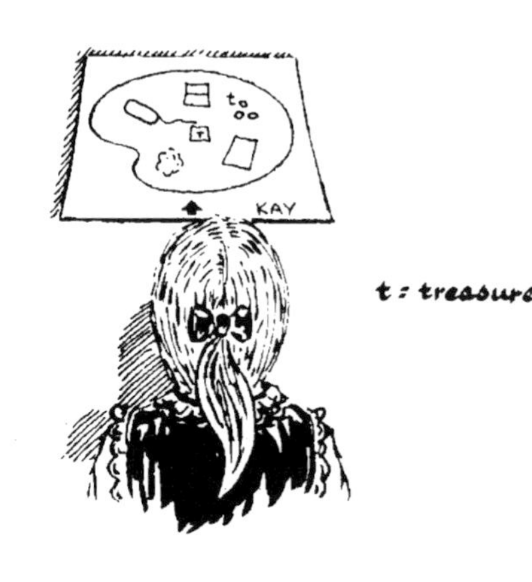

5. "Which route will you take to get to the treasure?" The leader demonstrates. Plan the route looking at the model, then trace it on the map with a finger or other pointer. The map must be kept set to follow the route. A few can talk through the route which they would follow, identifying the features they will pass by pointing at the model or the map.

6. If the island is big enough, the group members can then try to follow the route, walking from one feature to the next until the treasure is reached.

7. Add north, south, east and west to the model and maps, then use those terms to describe positions and routes, e.g. Kay sits between the south and east ends of the island, the house is in the north.

To proceed with the next exercises you may wish to purchase the specialist equipment and have some help in mapping an area. There are a number of professional and semi-professional mappers who will provide you with a finished product. Both mappers and suppliers of equipment can be contacted through the National Federations listed in Appendix 1.

ORIENTEERING STAR EXERCISE

EQUIPMENT
Boards, size approximately 20x20cm
Maps of the school and playground
8-10 mini-controls or coloured tapes
8-10 coloured wax crayons with string
Enlarged copy of map (approx A3) on board

OBJECTIVES
- *To introduce orienteering*
- *To find features (controls) which are out of sight using a large scale map*
- *To locate positions*
- *To practise and improve performance*
- *To undertake simple orientation activity*
- *Decision making*
- *To develop understanding of the following terms: ORIENTEERING, SET, CONTROL MARKERS*

Preparation
Plan 8-10 control sites, some within sight and others just out of sight of the base/start. Mark the controls on all the maps, including the enlarged version, with red circles. (Use a circle template.) Number each circle. Tape the maps to the boards. Hang the control markers and crayons at the controls.

Lesson
1. Give each person a map on a board. Go outside to the base shown as the triangle on the map. Set the map and discuss the features and symbols. The large A3 size map is useful for demonstrating how to set the map.

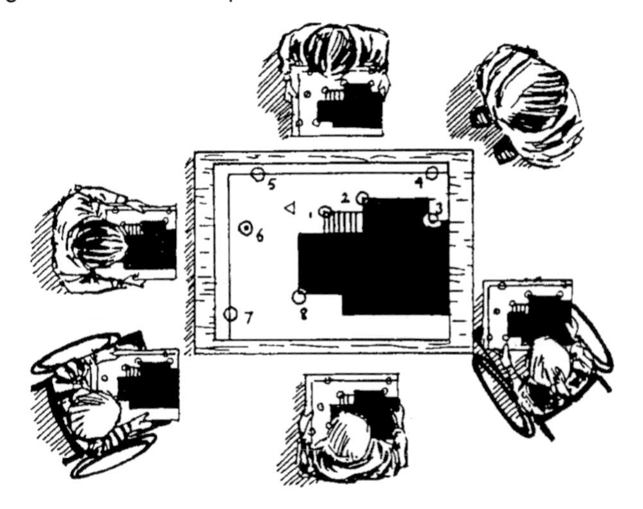

Identify (point out) a control. Set the map. Both the instructor and the participant move to the control. Repeat a few times, checking that everyone can set the map. Use a distinctive wall, hedge or road to help match the map to the ground. Point out the crayon hanging from the control.

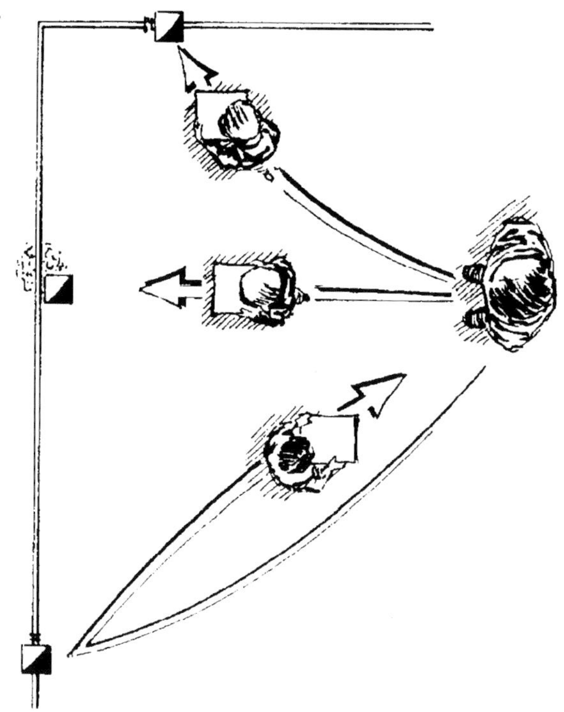

2. Star exercise: each person is given one control to find. They have to go to the control, colour in the right circle on the map with the crayon hanging there then return to base to join the queue ready to be told which is the next control to visit.

Before moving off those taking part should point out to the instructor the control flag he/she is going to, or, if it is out of sight, describe where it is.

Continue until most of the participants have all the circles coloured in. Check that the colours are correct.

Further work
Some members of the group could now go round the controls in a given order, marking control card boxes with the correct colour.

EQUIPMENT
6-8 mini-control markers (or coloured tapes) with wax crayons attached
A large (A3) map of the school and grounds
Small (A5) maps of the school and grounds with control boxes down one edge

OBJECTIVES
- *To remind the group that they should see the map as a picture*
- *To teach change of direction on the orientated map*
- *To practise orientation*
- *To practise locating their own position in relation to the landscape*
- *To recognise angles as a measurement of turn*
- *To develop understanding of the following terms: KEEP THE MAP SET, ORIENTEERING, ROUTE, ORIENTATION*

POINT TO POINT ORIENTEERING

Preparation

Plan 6-8 control sites. They should be mostly different from those used in the previous exercise. Mark all the control sites on all the maps with red circles. Mark the start/finish with a triangle. Highlight a strip down one edge of the map with a bright colour. This need not necessarily be North, rather a hedge or wall which will act as the main reference line for setting the map. Hang the controls and crayons.

Exercise

1. In the classroom: Evaluate the group's understanding of the playground map and the symbols used. Look at the large map of the school and ask individuals to identify specific features e.g "Which entrance do you use to come into the school?"; "Which area is used for play at break time?" Ask them to close their eyes and imagine what each feature looks like: "Make a picture of it in your head". This is how they should 'read the map'.

2. Outside: Start at the triangle. Set the map using the coloured edge to help. Lay the map on the ground in front of you, still set.

On the map, find the control with number "1" beside it. This is the first control. Move around the set map until you are looking in the direction of the control as viewed from the start. Pick up the map. The map is set. You are facing along the route you want to follow. DEMONSTRATE CLEARLY.

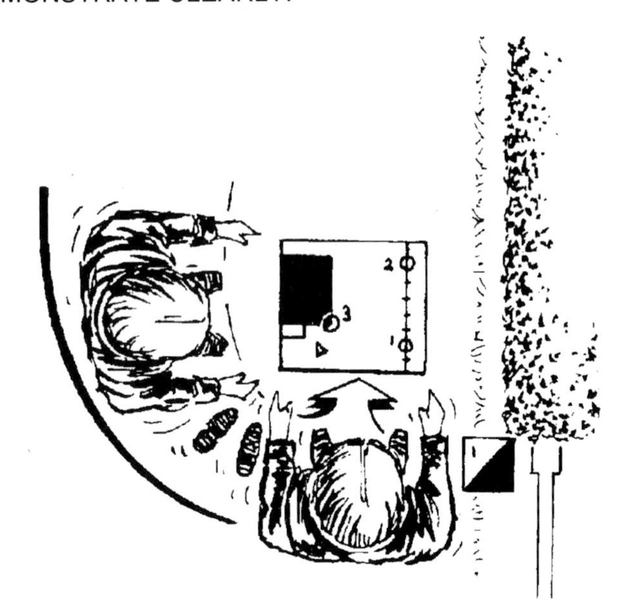

3. All go to control 1. Do not use the crayon. At each control follow this procedure:

- Set the map (on the ground, if this helps)
- Find the next control on the map. What is it?
- Move around the map until you are facing the right way.
- Look. Can you see the marker? If not, plan your route.

Promote individual decision making.

- Make up your own mind about which way you should face.

Send the group members round the course individually to practise this on their own. This time they should mark the control boxes with the coloured crayons. Start each person off as soon as the last has left the first control.

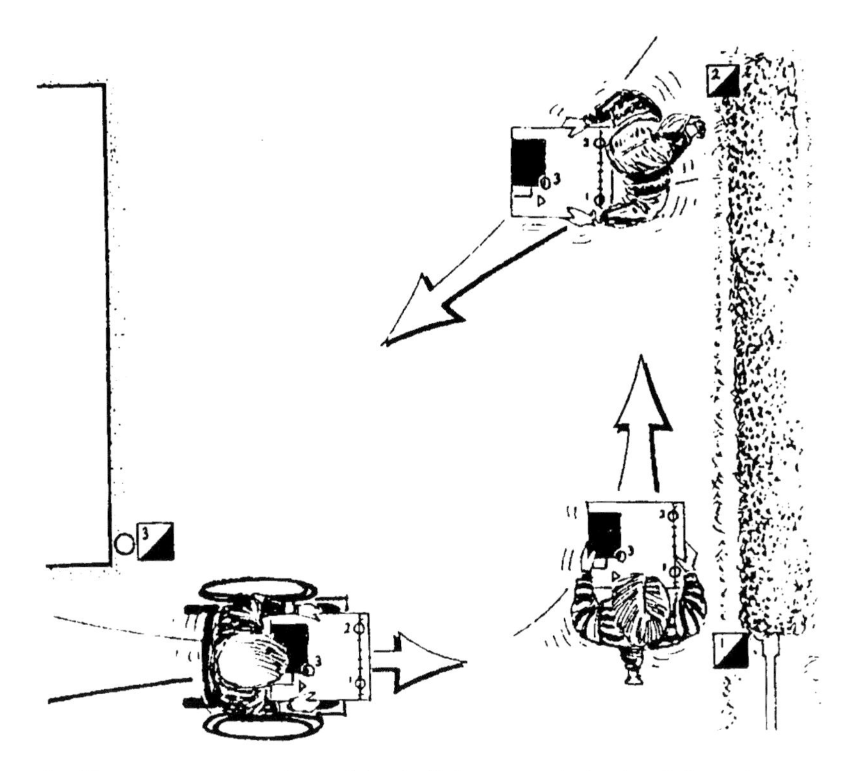

4. After each person has visited all the controls in the right order, send him/her round again. This time the circles on the map can be coloured in. Those needing extra help will have been identified by this time, and can be given more attention.

EQUIPMENT
Mini markers with numbers and code letters
Red crayons/pens
Playground maps
Pencils

OBJECTIVES
- *To introduce the new map*
- *To reinforce setting the map, orientation activity*
- *To help participants maintain contact with the map as they move about*
- *To improve performance through practice*
- *To develop understanding of the following terms: MAP CONTACT, SETTING THE MAP, STAR EXERCISE*

STAR EXERCISE

Preparation
This exercise is similar to the previous ones, using a map of a larger area, with controls further away from the base. Hang 8-10 mini-markers on definite features in the playground, school field or park. Make a master map and plan a route to include all the controls.

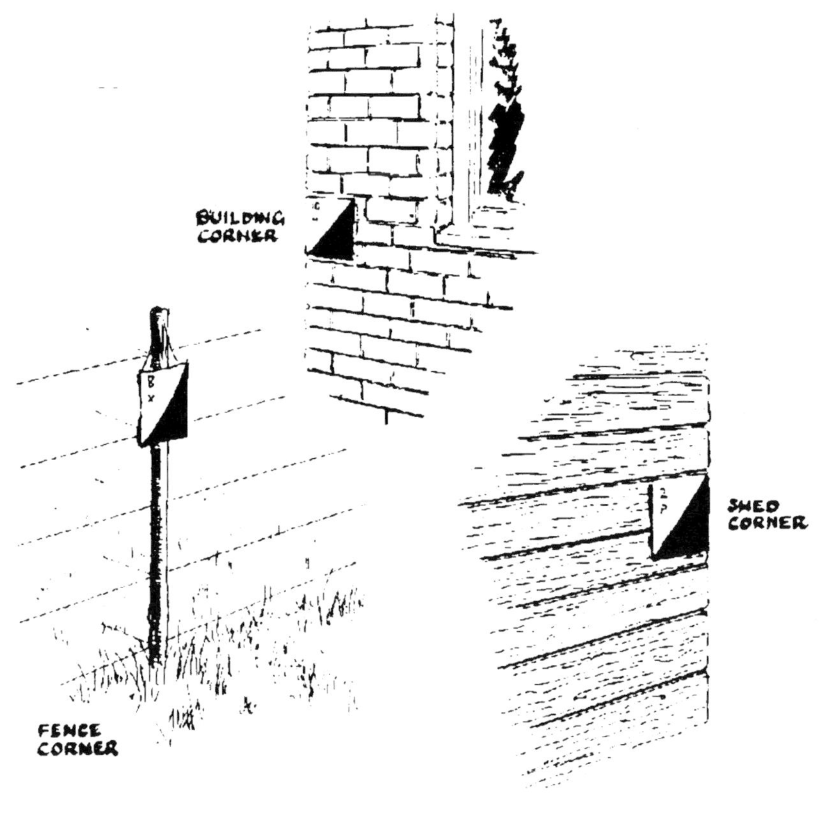

Practical

Using the map, take the group for a map 'walk'. Each person must have his/her own map. Insist that the map is correctly set and that evryone is able to point to their position on the map whenever they stop. NB Orienteers normally fold their maps and hold them with the thumb beside their last known position. This is part of keeping map contact.

During the 'walk', point out features and ask questions about map/terrain details. Ensure this is done slowly so that everyone is always aware of their position on the map. The 'walk' should lead past the mini markers which have been hung on definite features which are also on the map, e.g. 'fence corner' not just 'fence'.

At each marker the participant or an assistant on their instruction draws a circle on their maps in the correct place. Check that they get this exactly right. Number the circles.

Star exercise

This is one of the best orienteering exercises for teaching skills to mixed ability groups. Individuals can work at their own pace and the instructor is in contact with the whole group.

Photo: Glynn Roberts

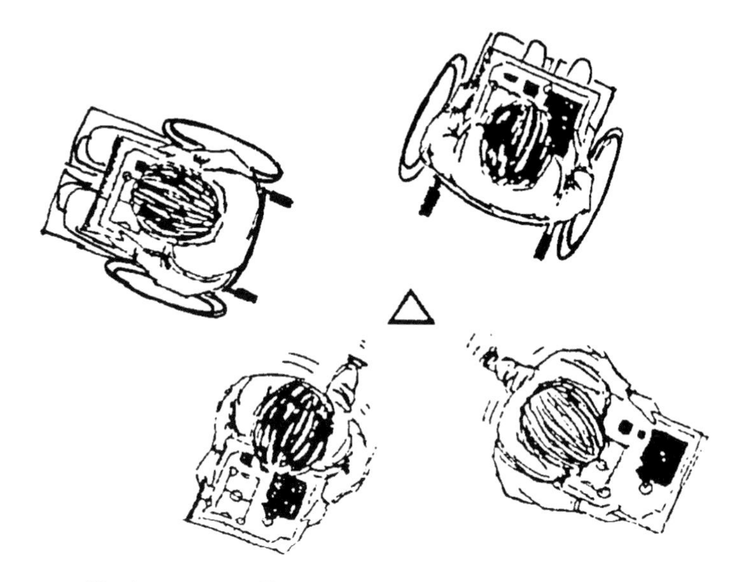

Each person will return to the base (triangle) after finding each control.

Number the participants to indicate which control each one is to find first, e.g. number 6 goes to control 6 first.

Emphasise that they must return after each control, remembering the code letter. This should be written down for checking on return to base.

Each time he/she returns to base, the map must be set with the person facing the right direction before going to the next control. The instructor can give help to those who need it.

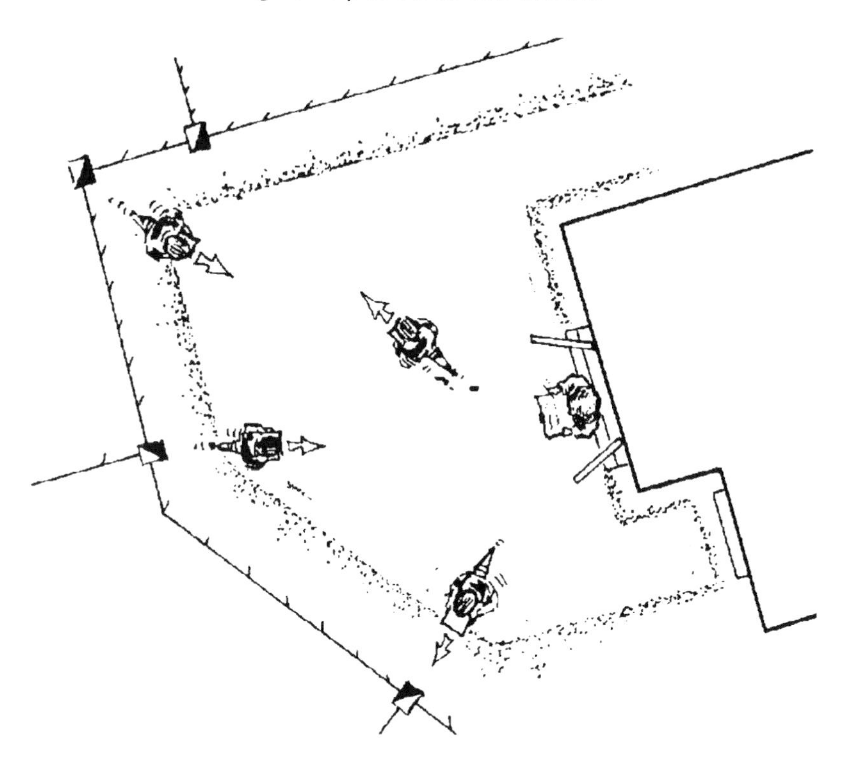

Having expanded their orienteering horizons to the limit of the home environment, the participants may now be ready to look beyond, to larger and more public areas and to exercises and events which will provide a more exciting challenge to the new orienteers - and give them an excursion as well. To take this next step, - one which brings them into the orienteering community proper - you will almost certainly need more help. The next chapter shows how to find it and what the results might be.

Chapter 6 Expanding Your Horizons

This chapter gives more background in using the tools of orienteering, the map and compass, and there is another practical exercise. People who have successfully completed this will not be classified as novices when they arrive at a competitive event and will be ready for the C (Rose) course, real Trail Orienteering. This exercise is of interest to teachers and organisers of group activities for a recreational, rather than competitive experience in the outdoors.

There are few parts of Britain far from areas with potential for some form of orienteering. Orienteers in the UK have had to use considerable imagination in order to find sufficient areas for the sport to flourish and grow. They relish competitions in mature forest rich in small contour detail, but almost every weekend you will find small, local events taking place quite satisfactorily on open heathland, dunes, old quarry workings, and in both country and town parks. Large parks in or near towns are in fact excellent training grounds for young and novice orienteers. They can be mapped at a large scale to show every bit of detail, and nearly always have a very definite boundary such as a wall or perimeter fence to 'catch' those who have gone a wee bit astray.

Having mentioned contour detail, this is a good place to explain a bit more about it.

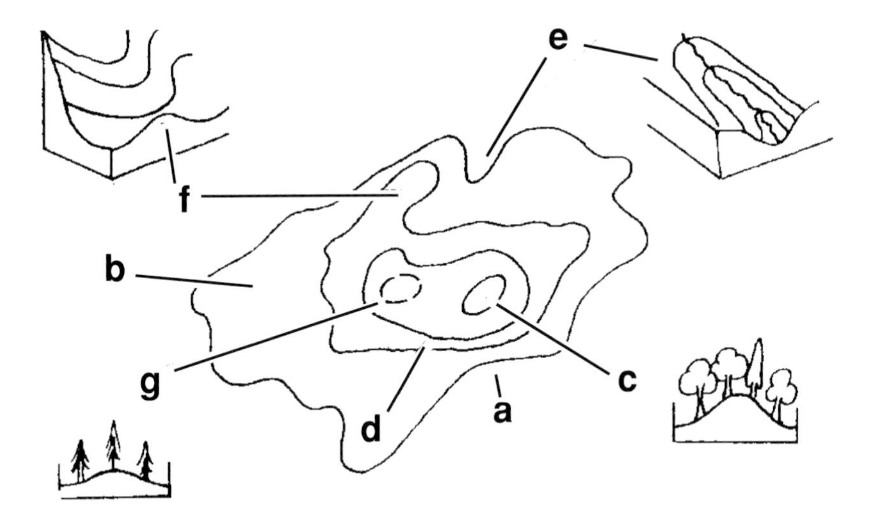

a: Contours close together show steep ground.
b: Contours spaced apart show a gradual slope or flatter ground.
c: A ring contour shows a hill top.
d: The more contours there are, the higher the hill.
e: A valley or re-entrant is shown by a bend in a contour pointing to the uphill side. It may or may not have a stream in it.
f: A spur or ridge is shown by a nose-shaped contour line.
g: A form line (intermediate contour) helps to improve the picture the map gives to the orienteer.

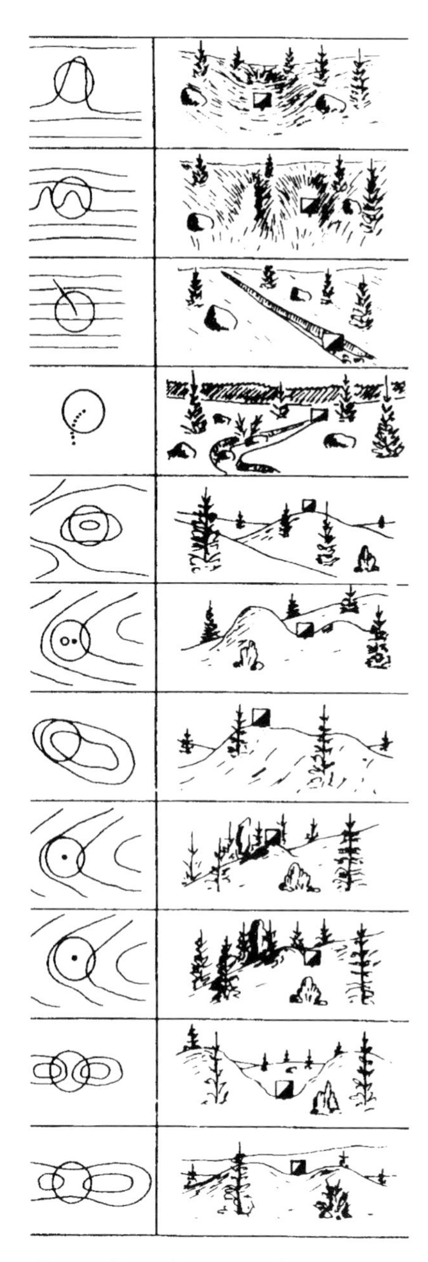

Examples of contour features

For disabled people too, parks hold much promise, not least because they very often have good networks of surfaced paths which can accept wheelchairs without difficulty. Courses of modest length but still providing much of interest can be devised with ingenuity and imagination (and incidentally, these are not bad training grounds for course planners and mappers either).

If you, the new orienteers have developed to the point where you have reached the limit of the recreation the home environment can provide, now's the time to call on the orienteering community to help. There are orienteering clubs in most parts of the country, and you can locate a contact address in a number of ways.

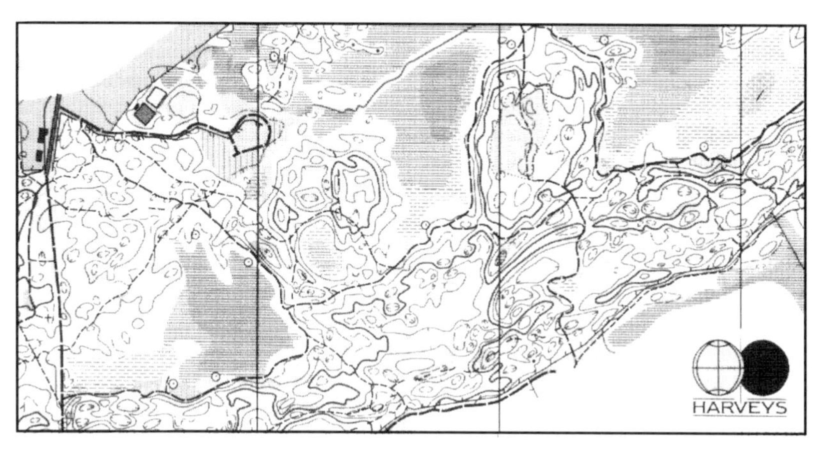

Try your nearest public library of reasonable size. They often hold lists of local clubs and associations, or contact your National Orienteering Federation (address in Appendix B).

Once you have made contact, ask someone from the club to come and talk to you about the possibility of getting courses suitable for disabled people incorporated into a local event, or perhaps of having a small event specially laid on in an already-mapped area. The club contact will know which areas in the vicinity are suitable and, just as importantly, which of them have been mapped, and what arrangements have to be made for access and insurance cover.

The most likely option, and in many ways the best, is for the club to put on, with your help, a small event specially for disabled orienteers, probably in a park with good paths. A spring or summer evening is a good time for such an event, and you may well find that club members have already done something similar. They will in any case have all the equipment needed for the event - control markers, cards, punches, banners and so on. If the club already has experience in dealing with disabled orienteers, so much the better - they will be aware of problems with eye-levels for people in wheelchairs and other such matters and will be ready to deal with them. If it's a new experience for both of you then perhaps you should get the club to buy a copy of this book! Information for event organisers appears in Part 2 which lists everything that needs to be taken into consideration for all levels of Trail O competition.

The actual organisation of the event can safely be left to the orienteering club, once you have decided how many courses you want, of what length, and any special needs that those taking part may have both with regard to actually tackling the course and with such things as the availability of suitable toilets. There may perhaps even be a mixture of orienteering courses for those with physical disabilities both ambulant or in wheelchairs, and a 'string' course or similar for people with learning difficulties. It is up to you to decide whether to try advertising the event around the disabled community. The first time out, you may prefer not to do this, but after that it could be fun to have others joining in.

Photo: Glynn Roberts

You may find that other disabled groups in the area are indeed interested in taking up orienteering. If so, you can combine with them in putting on events, which reduces the workload for everybody and also opens the possibility both of disabled people making new friends and of a certain amount of gentle rivalry between establishments.

The great value of a specially arranged event is that it acts as a 'halfway house' between the familiarity of games played in or around the home environment and the maybe daunting challenge of being part of a mainstream orienteering event with perhaps hundreds of other people taking part. Such an exercise may need to be repeated several times before both you (an activity organiser), or the new orienteers, feel ready to step fully into the orienteering community, and there is nothing wrong with that, especially if you can ring the changes by using a number of different areas.

Publicity may start to become an important issue at this point. If an event is being staged for the disabled, it is certainly worth contacting the local paper, who may well be interested enough to send a reporter and photographer along. Should a story be published, the power of the press may soon lead to other groups contacting you to find out more about this new sport!

Putting on events, even on a modest scale, takes a fair amount of time and effort, and as with most sports, those involved are volunteers. It helps enormously if an orienteering facility is available without the need to construct it. Such facilities do exist. They are called permanent courses, and the next chapter looks at how they are made and what purpose they serve.

EQUIPMENT
Pencils (on string)
Maps
Controls

OBJECTIVES
- *To encourage continuous map contact*
- *Thumbing the map*
- *Individual decision making*
- *Sustained running activity*
- *To specify locations and movement from angles on the map and route*
- *To develop understanding of the following terms: THUMBING, CONCENTRATION, MAP CONTACT*

LINE ORIENTEERING (practical exercise)

Preparation

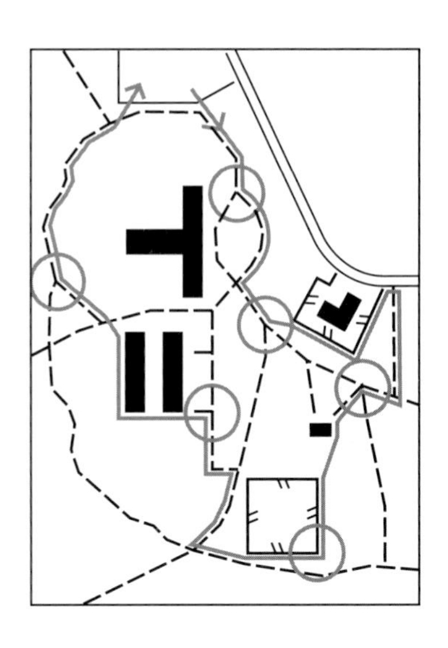

Plan a circular route following line features (mainly paths) with lots of changes of direction. This should be about 800m long, not more because of the level of concentration required to follow it. Put out 3-6 control markers at distinctive points along the route. The first control should be near the beginning of the line. Mark up the maps with a red line showing the route to be followed. Do not mark the controls on the map. People find this type of exercise quite hard because they are used to moving freely until they

see the marker. In this exercise they have to read the map all the time.

Assistant: Puts out controls. Helps children to follow the line.

Exercise

1. Use a short map 'walk' to familiarise the group with the map and surrounding terrain. Revise setting the map. Explain the purpose of the exercise. Each person will follow the route

shown by the red line on the map. If the route is followed correctly they will find control markers and can then mark the position of each control on the map. Show how to hold the map and trace progress with the thumb (thumbing). Assist those with limited physical control.

2. Thumb the start and take the whole group along the line to the first control. Mark the position of this control accurately on the maps.

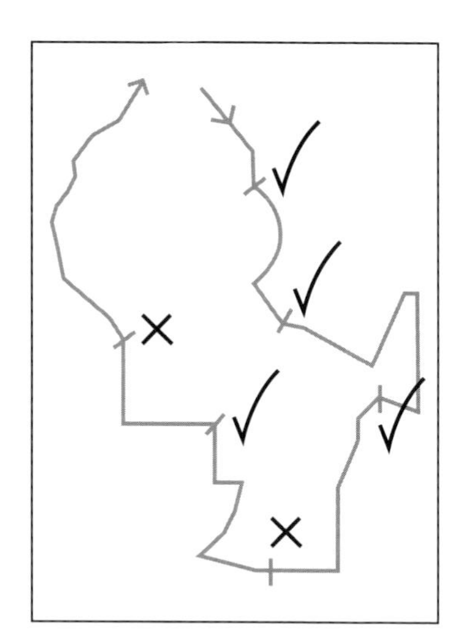

3. Allow the more able to continue on their own to the next control. If they mark that correctly then let them continue round to the finish and wait there. Continue behind with the remainder of the group sending them ahead as they become more competent and their confidence increases.

4. Check the maps to see if the controls have been marked accurately. Some may have made mistakes.

5. Go round the route again with the whole group together. Check that they are in contact with the map at each control marker.

INTRODUCING THE COMPASS

Stages of instruction

1. Establish NORTH. The magnetic needle always points north-south. Wherever you face, however you twist or turn, the compass needle always points to north.

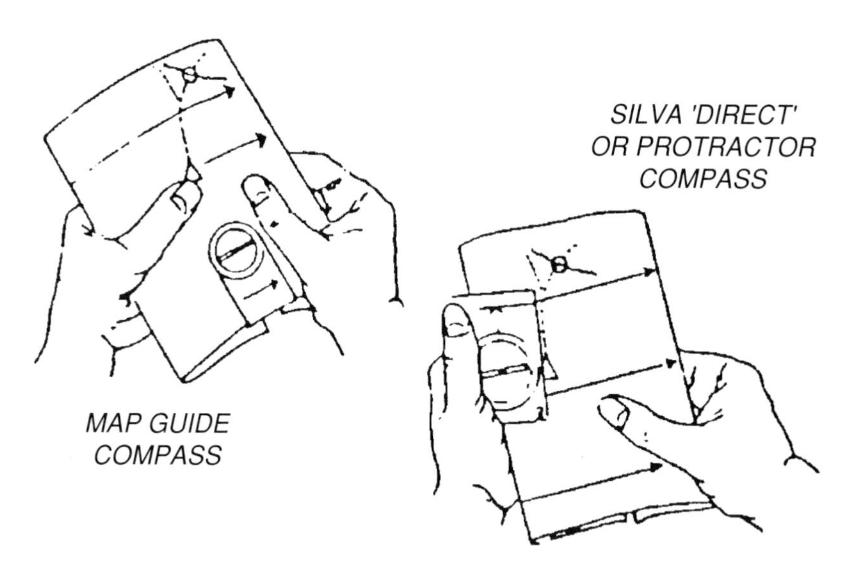

2. Fold the map square and small enough to 'thumb' your location. Hold the map so that you are looking straight along the route you want to take.

MAPGUIDE. Hold the map steady using two hands to 'steer'.

SILVA DNS 'DIRECT' or PROTRACTOR COMPASS. Hold the map and compass together with the edge of the compass alongside the route you want to take. Use both hands to keep compass and map steady.

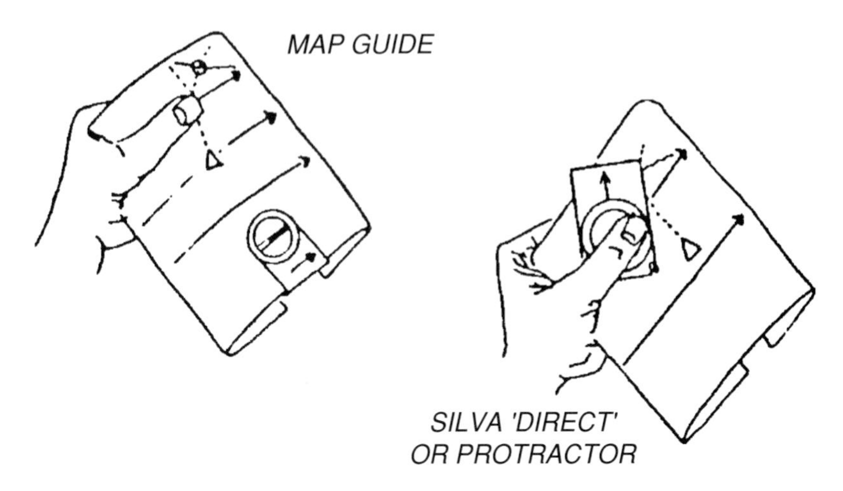

4. Turn yourself with map and compass fixed in front of you until the magnetic needle lies parallel to North-South lines on the map. Needle North = Map North.

5. You are now facing along the direction line you want to take. Take the spare hand away from the map: off you go! The DNS and protractor compass can be held in the opposite hand to the map if preferred.

6. Continue to read the map with your thumb. When the path changes direction - move your thumb - turn the map to look straight along the line you want to take - check that the Needle North points to Map North

Orientating and thumbing the map are the fundamental orienteering skills and should be constantly practised. Remember:

1. Every time a new orienteer uses a map in a practical situation, he or she should be sure it is orientated.

2. Competitors should develop the routine of checking that north on the compass corresponds with north on the map at every control point on a course and every time they stop and set off again en route.

In this way they can read off map details directly on the chosen route and on either side. Map and compass are used together in steering along the correct way.

Orienteering compasses

The compass is a direction finding instrument invaluable as an aid to precise navigation. Correct use will allow the orienteer to keep the map orientated in order to select routes and follow them faster while maintaining contact with the map. Maps used for orienteering have only magnetic North lines. This enables the compass to be used easily for map orientation.

Orienteers use different types of compass:

Map Guide Compass
This is designed and recommended to help the beginner to concentrate on looking at and thumbing the map, once it is orientated.

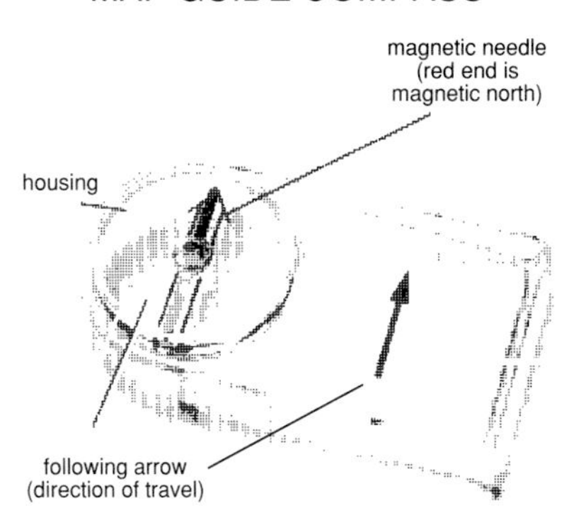

Silva Type 7DNS 'Direct' Compass
This is a much simplified version of the standard protractor compass, designed especially for children as a result of the Liverpool University Research Project into Children's Navigational Skills. It allows map orientation, direction checking and rough bearings to cut corners or aim off. It is ideal for beginners because the magnetic needle can be seen clearly within the housing and north on the compass dial is highlighted in red. When the red north-pointing magnetic needle matches the red N on the dial, all cardinal points and bearings can be read easily. Just remember, Red to Red for orientation. More sophisticated protractor compasses are available, but the 'Direct' compass allows basic skills to be learnt more easily.

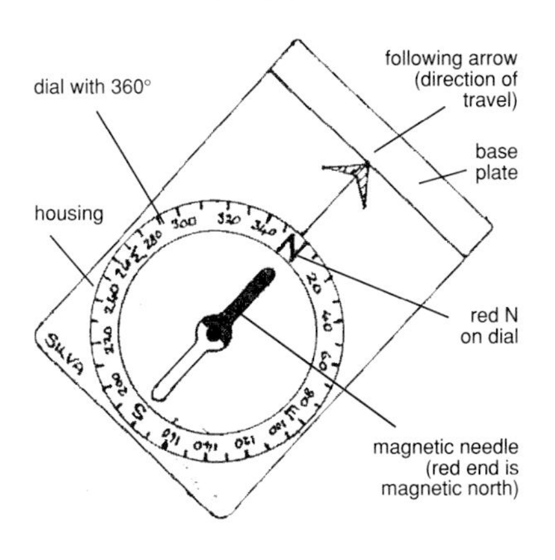

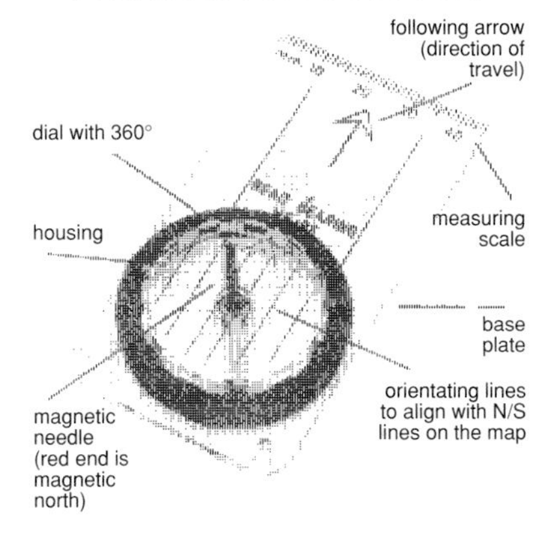

Protractor Compass
The protractor compass, like the 'Direct' compass can be used to take bearings as well as set the map. It requires careful teaching and considerable practice to use this compass accurately.

It is important that whichever compass is chosen it is used in the correct way.

Chapter 7 Permanent Courses

In Britain in recent years, a network of 'permanent courses' has been established. They have been set up by local authorities, Forest Enterprise or commercial forestry companies, outdoor pursuits centres, or individual landowners, acting in co-operation with orienteering clubs. Leaflets giving details of currently available courses and giving constructional guidelines can be obtained from the British Orienteering Federation.

What are permanent courses, and how usable are they by disabled orienteers? Permanent courses consist of a number of markers placed in an interesting area at clearly identifiable points. The markers remain in place for long periods, years in fact, thus providing to all intents and purposes a permanent opportunity for practising skills, or introducing people to orienteering. People using permanent courses decide themselves which markers to visit and in what order, but suggestions are sometimes given on which combinations make for interesting or challenging courses. Permanent course orienteering is thus not a variation of a waymarked nature trail but a form of the sport without the competitive element.

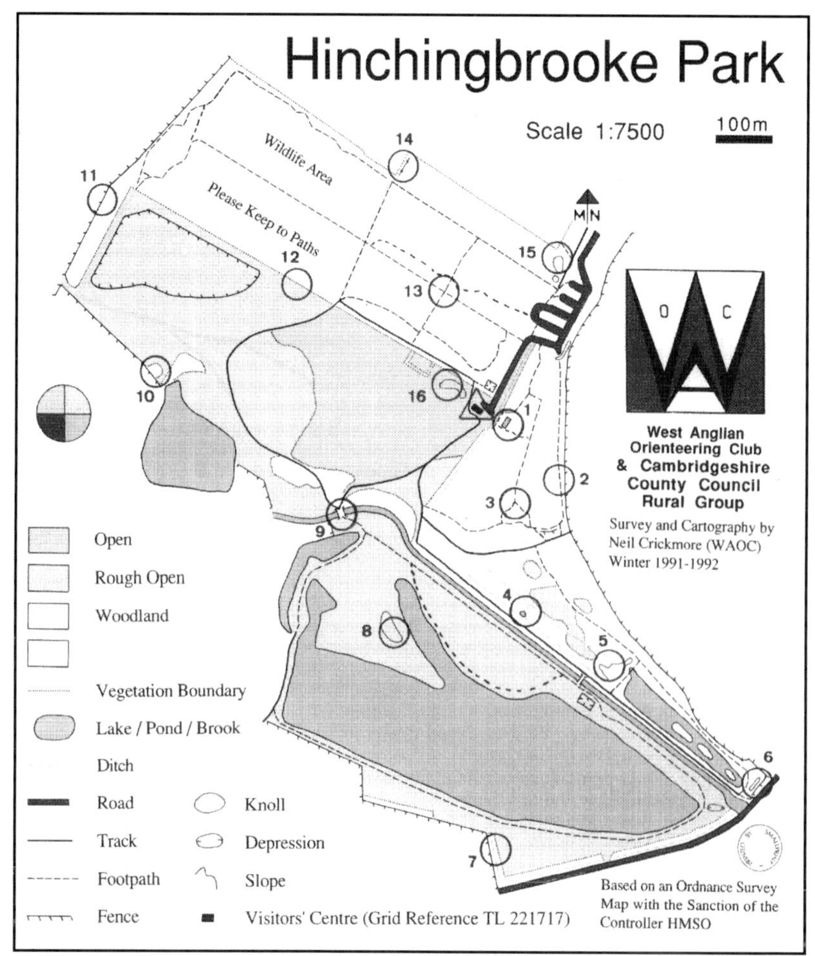

The markers may be wooden posts set in the ground or wooden, metal or plastic plates attached to buildings or other mapped features. Each marker displays the standard orienteering symbol together with a code. Sometimes a horizontal arrow shows magnetic north to help you set or realign your map.

Everybody using the course should receive a pack of information. It should include an orienteering map of the area, overprinted with the positions of the markers; a sheet of 'control descriptions' and codes. Usually some general information is provided about orienteering and local clubs.

Permanent courses are often found in town or country parks, on local areas of heath or moorland, or in small woods. Some permanent courses, though not necessarily all the control sites within them, will certainly be suitable for use by disabled people, and your local orienteering club or local authority leisure services department will be able to advise on this. It must be borne in mind that it is not usually possible to reserve exclusive use of the course, so your visit may coincide with that of other orienteering groups, perhaps a school or scout group introducing young people to the sport. This should not create a problem and indeed may even provide you with extra helpers!

Because they are in public places and are necessarily left unattended (though regular checks are carried out), permanent courses may attract the attention of people whose main aim is to spoil the enjoyment of others by removing or defacing markers and other equipment. If you come across such damage, please do report it as soon as possible to whoever administers the course.

One advantage of permanent courses is their flexibility. You can do your own simple course planning to suit the abilities of those taking part and the amount of time you have available.

It may be that there is no permanent course in your area. In this case you might like to campaign for one to be set up. It can be quite a lengthy and time-consuming business getting all the necessary permissions, making or acquiring the equipment and so on, but at the end of it you would have your own local orienteering facility.

There is, at the time of writing, one permanent Trail Orienteering course in Britain, at Whinlatter in the Lake District. Richard Warner, who was closely involved in setting it up, has written a fascinating account of how it came about, which we reprint here with his permission, and the hope that landowners will consider a permanent orienteering course when developing leisure facilities.

The Whinlatter Story

A permanent orienteering course at Whinlatter has been available since 1980, and the Calvert Trust (a holiday centre for the disabled, catering for a variety of outdoor pursuits) has used part of it since 1987. They would transport wheelchairs to the top of the forest and then set off downhill, racing to the bottom - a descent of some 1200 feet in about three miles which I'm told was exciting, to say the least! More by luck than judgement, this particular route passed nine of the permanent markers, thereby creating the equivalent of an orienteering course.

In 1990, Sue Kysoe, a member of West Cumberland Orienteering Club then working for the Calvert Trust, asked if we could design something more 'mentally challenging'. She supplied us with some information on what we now know to be Trail Orienteering and left us to it. Unfortunately, their route through the forest not only coincided with the easiest of our suggested permanent courses but also with the forest trail network, and it was felt that to add another 30 or so markers in the area would only lead to mass confusion. The idea was therefore shelved.

Then, in the winter of 1990-91, a series of gales laid waste the valley of Grisedale Gill. The valley sits at the head of an important 'conservation corridor', and the Forest Managers saw the damage as an opportunity to complete this corridor through to the open fell. The Forest Officer, Gareth Browning, then came up with the idea of a 'mountain arboretum'. This would be the first of its kind in England, and there was money available for this kind of prestigious project. But mountain arboretums take many years (and possibly many changes in management) to develop and so, in order to prevent the valley being returned to commercial forest, it was necessary to make it very special.

Photo: Viv Fowler

Over the years, our aim at Whinlatter has always been to encourage as many people as possible into the 'great outdoors', but a major stumbling-block has been our inability to cater for the less able. Gareth contacted the Calvert Trust to discuss the possibility of a 'disabled walk' around the valley. They jumped at the idea and immediately raised the subject of orienteering, at which point the British Orienteering Federation were contacted to see what was required.

Gareth then approached the head ranger, Mike Pearson, and myself with the proposal, and found that we already had some idea of what was needed. Once it was clear that the whole project could be done 'in house', management were quick to endorse it, and the ball was set in motion. WCOC had just got into computer mapping and they supplied us with the necessary software. Producing the map on computer proved to be of great benefit as we have been able to print a draft copy complete with the course which we are now running. The feedback over the first six months will be used to modify both the map and the course where necessary. The map is at 1:5000 scale.

Out in the forest, work was already well underway towards the arboretum, with most of the damaged trees removed and the ground tidied up, but the work had left the forest tracks in a very rough condition. Again the Calvert Trust were brought in, and they advised on gradients and surface and in particular the alignment of a new path and bridge needed to complete the trail. A kerb (actually a low earth mound) was raised along those sections of track which have steep drops beside them. A car park and picnic area was provided and we hope in the future to add a disabled toilet.

Armed with a computer printout map, we went around the area setting the control markers into position. During this process, not only were some of the markers placed to suit the map, but the map was altered to suit the markers! With the course finalised, a series of benches were placed at strategic points - at most of the markers and at the top of every incline. These have been appreciated by all those attempting the course as, despite all the hard work by the foresters, the route must still be graded as strenuous.

That is roughly how it happened. The following is a list of some of the ideas and intentions I tried to follow while designing the course:

1: The course had to be completely isolated from both the forest trails and the existing permanent orienteering course - both to avoid confusion and to deter vandalism (school parties are notorious for removing markers!).

2: All markers had to be visible from a level viewing area. Parking a wheelchair on a slope is no fun.

3: All markers had to be visible from a seated position.

4: As many different control descriptions as possible were used, to avoid boredom and to introduce as many aspects of mapreading as we could.

5: Markers were placed so that the markers for each control site could have a variety of descriptions, thus making possible different levels of skill.

6: Letters on markers had to be large enough (3 inches/8cm) to be easily read.

7: Within reason, the course should start easy and get progressively harder. It is our intention to provide two courses here but by using this method, cover a broad range of skill levels. I feel that without the pressures of time to panic the brain, Trail O participants will reach a high level of skill far sooner than their counterparts in mainstream orienteering. Feedback so far seems to confirm this.

8: For the visually impaired, a map at twice the scale (1:2500) should be made available. Using computer mapping this is not a problem, though having two maps does increase printing costs.

We hope that Whinlatter will provide the inspiration for many other permanent courses for disabled orienteers. If it can be done in such relatively difficult terrain it can certainly be done in easier areas such as town parks, thus providing great opportunities for many more people to enjoy the pleasures of orienteering.

We are now ready to discuss true competitive Trail Orienteering, another substantial step up the orienteering ladder.

Chapter 8 Competitive Trail Orienteering

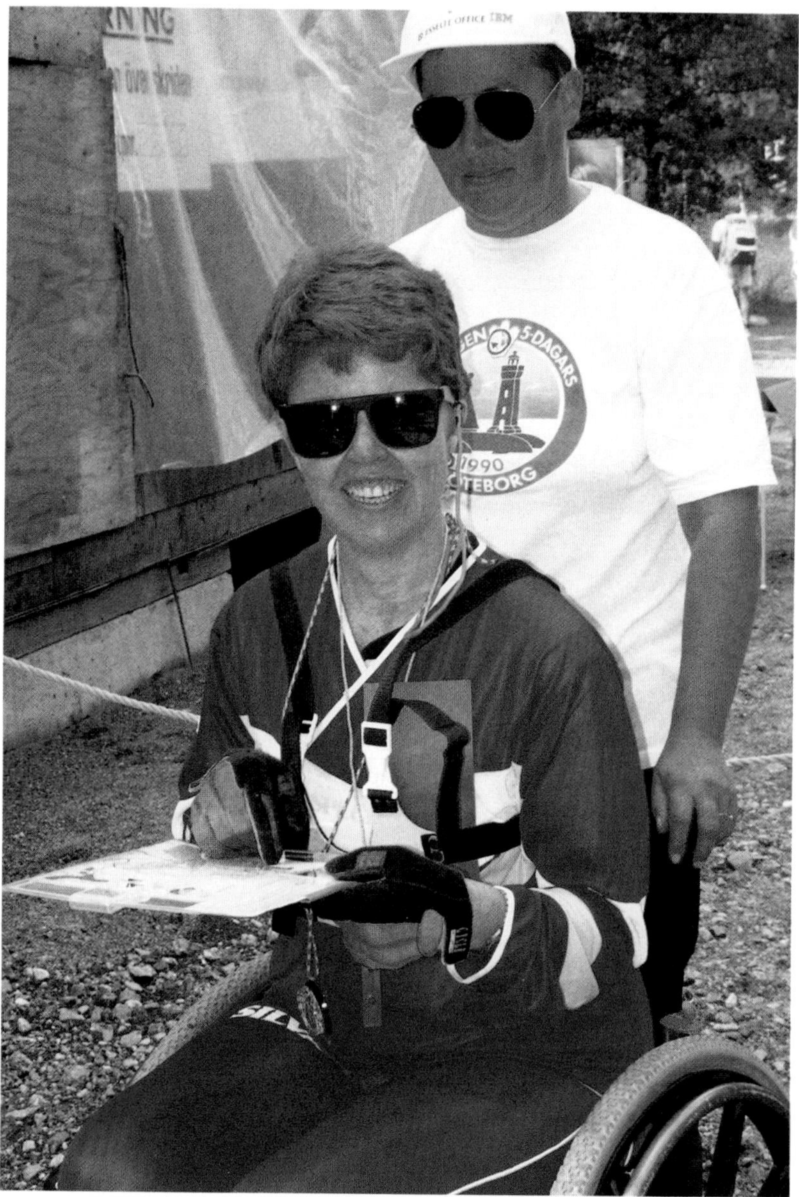

Photo: Camilo de Mendonca

In Chapter 4 we described a novice course, here we move on to competitive orienteering for disabled people, which has become known by the generic term of 'Trail Orienteering' or 'Trail O' for short. It was developed in Sweden as 'multichoice orienteering with false controls', one of many experimental versions and now considered to offer the fairest competition, allowing those with disabilities to compete on equal terms.

Events take several months to plan and organise, and the weather does not always co-operate. In case conditions are bad competitors should have suitable warm and waterproof clothing, or other form of protection, with them, possibly even a change of clothing and shoes.

Equipment required by the competitor is minimal and event organisers will most likely have some available for loan. A board to which the map can be attached is an advantage for competitors who need their hands to propel a wheelchair or hold a stick or crutches. There are two models normally available; one fits under the cushion of a wheelchair, the other, designed primarily for ski orienteering straps round the chest. Both can have a basic compass attached. This will be quite adequate for the beginner. The experienced Trail orienteer will need a protractor compass.

The format of Trail O is similar to mainstream orienteering, but with some significant differences in the way the actual competitive element is arranged. Most courses are more suited to people with the visual and mental capacity to interpret the symbols, to read and understand the map and relate it to the terrain, and to move on foot or in a wheelchair which may be pushed or power-driven. There are moves to organise courses for visually handicapped people, but in 1993 they are at an early stage. For those with learning difficulties,

Photo: Don Braggins

the string course has already been mentioned, as has the idea of running with a buddy on an appropriate colour-coded course.

There will be a course suitable for novices, but those who have followed some of the exercises in the proceeding chapters will wish to start on the Rose or C course.

One fundamental difference is that Trail O competitors are not timed around the course from start to finish as happens at most orienteering events. Nor are competitors disqualified for marking the wrong box at controls. Instead, they score points for identifying controls correctly, and the possible total number of points scored around the course is reduced for each error. Decision-making, which is fundamental to all orienteering, is thus still present, but less in route choice and more in control identification. Trail O competitors may receive physical assistance at any stage, but no help with the decision-making.

At registration you may be asked if you are eligible (through a disability) for the restricted group or if you wish to compete in the open section. The two participate together and the results are comparable, but in top competition there may be separate awards.

The role of helpers

Some disabled competitors will be able to complete the course without any help, but others will require some assistance - eg someone to push a wheelchair. In most circumstances it is desirable that they are accompanied around the complete course.

For these purposes the orienteering club and/or the disabled group may approach local PE/community sports students, scouts or guides. Alternatively escorts, helpers and friends accompanying the disabled competitors can be used. For reasons of fairness, helpers for the A and E classes should be allocated by the event organiser and not be a member of the same orienteering club as the competitor, nor their 'escort'.

Some competitors may be physically unable to mark their own cards, and in such cases the person accompanying them round the course may do so by following their instructions.

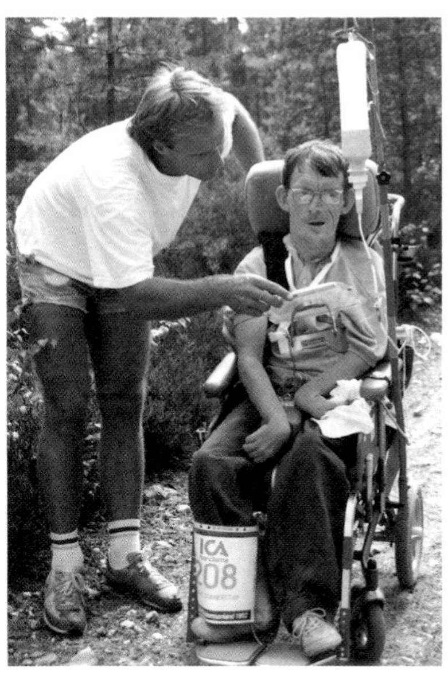

Photo: Camilo de Mendonca

The Trail O Event

The competitor receives a map with the start, the positions of the controls and the finish already printed on it, together with a sheet of control descriptions, normally the pictorial type used internationally in orienteering.

In addition to the correct marker shown by the centre of the control circle, others may be placed in the terrain near the correct one (see Illustration). The positioning of these 'false' controls is

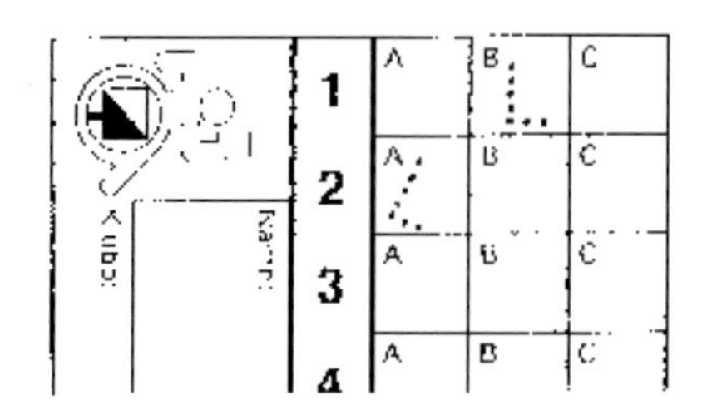

explained in the section on courses. The competitor's task is to decide which control in the terrain corresponds with the one marked on the map. All competitors (whether in wheelchairs or not) will be required to stay on the path to identify the correct control. Competitors normally carry a punch used to mark the control card, thus indicating which of the control markers in the terrain, in the competitors opinion, correctly represents the feature shown by the centre of the circle on the map and on the accompanying control description sheet. The special control cards used for Trail Orienteering (see illustration) thus have multiple choice boxes (usually labelled A, B, C etc) for each control. Near each control site there is a viewing or decision-making point identified by a card giving the course and control number, e.g. N3 or A6. Competitors may move up and down the track to view the control markers but need to return to the viewing point to decide how to mark the card.

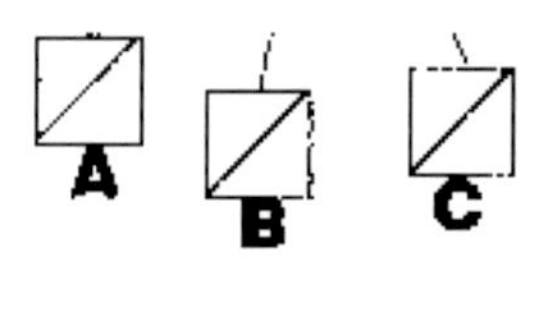

The control marker farthest to the left as seen from the viewing point, is deemed to be A and those to the right of it B, C etc. Competitors simply indicate by punching the correct box on the control card which control marker they think accords with the centre of the circle on their map - A, B, C, D etc. Larger integrated events are likely to use the logo illustrated below left to distinguish Trail O control markers from any others in the terrain.

With the alternative control card, used mainly at introductory or 'home' organised events, an indicator card will be placed at the viewing point to show the box numbers for punching. Competitors are issued with a pair of cards fixed together with clear sticky tape. At the finish they will have one card returned, so that they can compare it with the 'master card' on display.

Thus, in Trail Orienteering, a point is scored for each correctly punched box, and the competitor who has the highest number of correctly punched boxes is the winner.

Trail O Classes

At Trail O events, a number of classes will normally be provided. There is no class division by age, sex or type of disability and courses will in most cases be open to those recovering from an injury, unfit or others who cannot or do not wish to compete on timed courses over rough terrain.

The colours mentioned below are used in Britain. They may be different in other countries.

For the novice (N) class, the cream course should be planned as a 'failsafe' first experience giving competitors an opportunity to interpret the special maps but with little chance of failing to complete the course correctly. Such a course is described in Chapter 4. Helpers may give assistance in interpreting the map for novices. In Britain, novice courses may well be linked with the easy introductory white or yellow courses at colour-coded events.

With the C class, the rose course provides the next step forward, catering for those who have already seen and tried Trail Orienteering, but planned so that competitors are likely to complete the course having made very few wrong decisions. At each control site there will be one false control marker but on a very different feature to the correct one.

For B class competitions, the sky course will have control sites on major features within 20m or so of the path, and two false controls at each site.

The A and E classes are intended to attract ex-competitive orienteers as well as those with disabilities who wish to compete at more advanced levels and who have shown good navigational skills gained by experience. A fawn course should be provided for A class competitors who will need to understand relief.

Photo: Angela Whitworth

Control markers will be hung on more difficult features than in the B class and as long as they can be clearly seen from the path, may be 40 or more metres distant. 'Parallel features' - two similar features such as gullies, streams or knolls close together on the map - may be used (and are in fact desirable). Competition in the E class on a grey course demands even better understanding of map and terrain and requires advanced compass bearing techniques.

Up to five control markers will be at each control site on an 'E' course, none of which need be on the feature depicted by the centre of the control circle. There is no numbered stake at the viewing point, the competitor must determine whether they are looking at the right set of control markers and place themselves in the correct position, this is where control marker A (the left one) is at 90° from the track. If it is concluded that no control marker is on the feature the decision is recorded by punching the control card in the blank box.

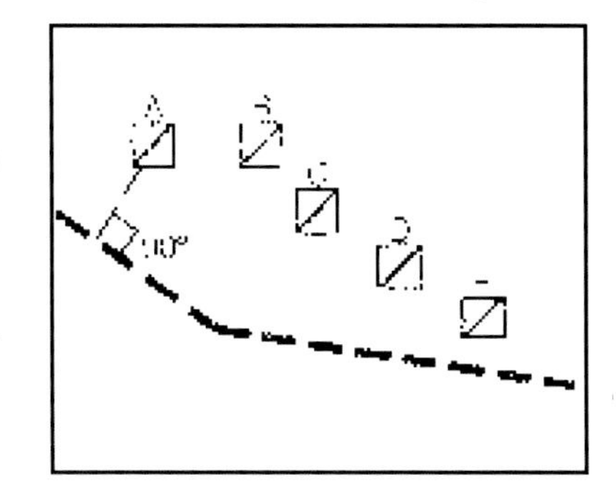

Timed controls

In conventional competition, timing to the nearest second establishes the finishing order. With Trail O a number of competitors may have the same score, and for more advanced categories of competitor a 'tie-break' method has been established using timed controls. The time taken is that used in decision-making and not in movement.

On arrival at the timed control viewing-point, the competitor is asked by a marshal to assume a designated position. He or she is then asked if all the control markers are visible, and instructed on the procedure for answering. The control on the left is designated A, the next along B, and so on. Competitors should be made aware (a) that these controls are used as tiebreakers, (b) of the penalty clause (a wrong answer or no answer involves a one minute time penalty) and (c) that there is a time limit (usually 2 minutes). All controls should be visible without the need for much movement. The lack of physical mobility must not introduce an element of unfairness.

When ready, the competitor is handed (or has placed on a map stand) a correctly orientated map with the control description at the top and one control circle marked. A stopwatch is started as the map is handed over, and stopped immediately the site is named; both the answer and the time taken are recorded on the competitor's control card using a waterproof pen or soft pencil.

Drawing: Guthrie Hutton

Time Allowance

The overall time taken to complete the course is largely irrelevant, though a time limit can be set which, if exceeded, will incur penalty points. This is only likely to affect the A or E competitor who has up to 3.5 km and 25 controls, and must learn to limit the time taken at each control.

Results

Once a Trail O competitor has completed the course, the control card is checked against a master card held by the organisers. Checking involves ensuring that punchmarks are in the correct boxes, totalling those correctly recorded and calculating the time taken at the timed controls. The winner is the competitor with the highest number of correctly punched controls and (in the event of a tie) the shortest elapsed time taken at the timed controls. A correctly punched card should be displayed in the finish area.

Provisional results are displayed as quickly as possible at orienteering events, and are eagerly awaited by all competitiors.

Discussing the results and the map is an important part of the day and adds to the enjoyment of the competition.

Photo: Don Braggins

Chapter 9 Some Alternatives

During the development of Trail O some other forms of competition were tried. Although now considered to introduce some discrimination during competition they may be valid as training exercises, or to provide variation.

Line Events

A line event provides an interesting alternative competition for the more experienced competitors and is a valuable training exercise. A line is accurately drawn on the competitor's map between the start and the finish. It winds in the terrain on either side of the path to be followed by the competitors

Control markers are placed on the line or near to it. Points are scored for punching the control card box when a marker is on the line and for leaving blanks where one that is not on the line is passed.

Swedish line event map

For the most experienced competitors the line may be printed as broken. The lack of control descriptions adds to the difficulty of this type of orienteering.

The accuracy of overprinting the courses is vital to fair competition and as the line normally needs to be drawn freehand it is a considerable task. The planner may be able to make and use a stencil. Alternatively a master map may be drawn up, with colour photocopies being used for the competitors. It is assumed that the centre of the line drawn with a fine pen represents the line in the terrain.

SCORE EVENT

CONTROL DESCRIPTIONS

Time limit - 30 minutes

5 point penalty
for every minute late

Each control punched
scores 10 pts

1	Fence, east end
2	Corner of trees
3	Path junction
4	Flower bed, south end
5	Climbing frame
6	Copse, SE edge
7	Building, NE corner
8	Monument
9	Wall, NW corner
10	Flower bed, N end
11	Clearing, E end
12	Wood edge
13	Fence corner
14	Trees, N end
15	Fence corner
16	Bank foot
17	Clearing, S corner
18	Hedge, N end
19	Pond, S edge
20	Pylon

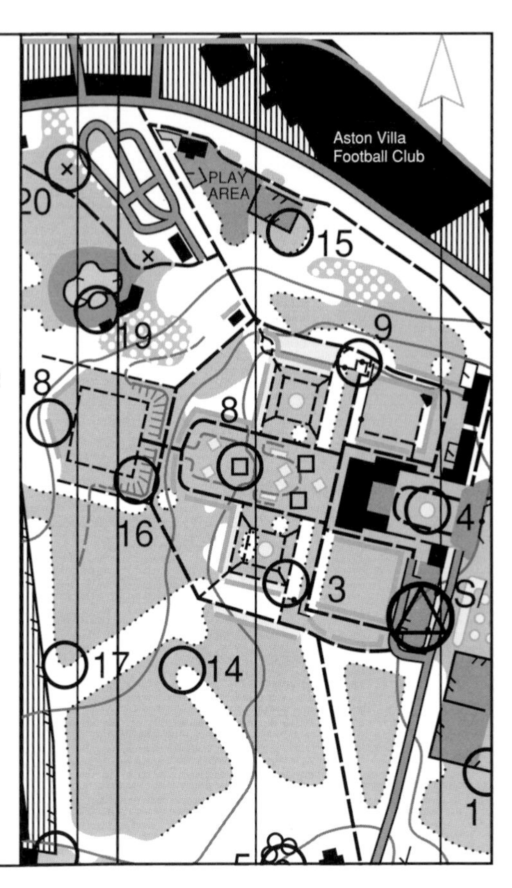

Score events

A score competiton is where the competitor visits as many control sites as possible in a given time. This introduces an element of route choice, something which is largely missing from other Trail O competitions. When organising a score event care must be taken with the map - areas which are impassable for wheelchairs (steps, for example) must be shown. Inevitably this type of event emphasizes the difference between disabilities and between kinds of wheelchair, as does the difference between the fast 21-year-old and the far slower 10 or 60 year old in Foot O score events.

Control markers will have codes and have punches associated with them, and must be accessible to wheelchair users and other competitors unable to manage rough terrain.

Sprint events

This is a version of the multi-choice event, with false controls. However, instead of one to four timed controls on the course, many of the controls will have the decision making timed. This adds a sense of urgency to the competition, and as a wrong answer incurs penalty points, pure guesswork cannot provide a winner.

Pin Point Orienteering

In this case the competitor has a map without any overprinting and no control description sheet or control card. The competitor follows a path (there will be no alternative route) and marks the map by inserting a pin at any point where a control marker is sited. This requries considerable manual dexterity and a soft mapboard.

Team Competition

Although most orienteering is an individual sport there are occasions when team competition is desirable. In this case the scores and times of a predetermined number of competitors, with those competitors competing either on the same course or a number of different courses, can be added together giving a club, school or other group result.

Night Events

The competition may also take the form of a night event. The control markers should have reflective tape attached and be carefully sited to ensure visibility.

'Marathon' Events

Marathon events are more akin to ski orienteering and will not be applicable for all. They are however a valid alternative that may be added to other courses if the area is suitable. The condition of the track needs to be better, and usually tarmac as the competitors will travel faster. Control sites will normally be similar to those used on the B course and the distance from 10km to 15km.

Chapter 10 Conclusion

To the participant

Now you have read this book we look forward to meeting you at events. We have stimulated your interest in this new discipline of Trail Orienteering and welcome all, but particularly those whose physical disabilities make participation, let alone top competition, in most sports impractical. We know you will appreciate the beautiful areas of countryside used for orienteering competition, and the company of other orienteers.

Photo: Don Braggins

Part 2

Chapter 11 For Organisers and Planners

Chapter 8 deals with competitive Trail O. Some additional information with points which may be of help to organisers and planners appear in this chapter.

The Season

It is recommended that in Britain most Trail O events should take place between April and October, thus avoiding the colder and more severe weather. The exact season will vary depending on geographical location and on the prevailing weather pattern.

Unsuitable terrain for Trail O

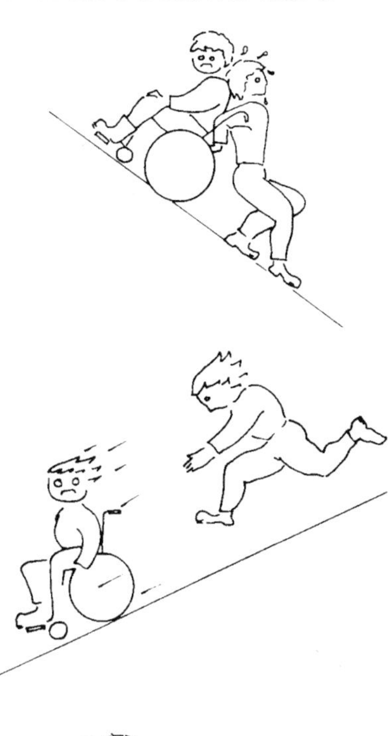

Drawings: Guthrie Hutton

Trail O Terrain

Trail O courses can be successfully planned on various types of terrain, but whatever terrain is used, it must be navigable by wheelchair competitors who can be pushed by escorts or additional helpers. The areas likely to be most appropriate are those with a good network of roads, tracks and wide paths, and perhaps grass fields. Steep terrain is generally unsuitable, although some contour detail is required for good planning on A and E classes. Fortunately, paths often follow contour lines, and steepish sections, if not too long, can be negotiated with the help of extra pushers stationed there for the duration of the competition. Many of the country parks in or around our major towns and cities make excellent venues, especially for introductory events.

Visibility from the path into the terrain (from wheelchair height) is important especially during spring and summer when new growth can easily hide the markers. Control sites that are relatively near to the path (up to 60m) are usually essential. Competitors must stay on the path, or on a few occasions follow a taped route, because an unfair advantage may be gained by ambulant competitors if they go closer to the controls by leaving the path. An unsuitable path, with steps, for example, will be shown by one or more crosses (XX) on the map and may have tapes across its starting point in the terrain.

As courses are unlikely to exceed 3.5km, a large area is not a requirement and many fine, challenging areas often have paths and tracks close to car parks. Mineral extraction sites may be good too, as they often have much contour detail.

We recognise that the condition of paths and tracks is vitally important. If they are covered in loose gravel or contain large stones, they can present a hazard. If they are very muddy they also cause difficulty, although the more experienced competitors enjoy the challenge. Obstacles such as gates, fences, stiles and cattle grids can limit the area available. With consultation it may be possible to bridge or temporarily remove such obstacles, and pushers can assist in negotiating short sections (up to 100 metres) of uneven or difficult surface. However, organisers must always remember that they are not supposed to be providing a challenge for wheelchair manufacturers, but an enjoyable outdoor activity.

Vinyl flooring sheet or similar material (even old carpet) can be laid over rough stretches of path, and moderate earth moving and consolidation can improve the short-term situation. Paths can be widened by cutting back overlong undergrowth (with permission, of course).

Photo: Anne Braggins

Publicity

For many years to come, the Trail O organiser will have a marketing, PR and publicity role prior to the event, notifying the press and disability organisations in the area and if at all possible visiting the latter with a video and other material to explain how orienteering can be offered. Reminders should be sent out three or four weeks before the event, and final details circulated. Even then, if the weather is poor, attendances may be low.

Facilities for Trail O

Parking

Car parking is a key factor at any orienteering event, and lack of suitable facilities has been known to prohibit use of an area. It is essential for disabled competitors to be able to park adjacent to registration. A number of vehicles such as mini-buses adapted to carry wheelchairs, may need to find suitable parking, and it may be necessary to reserve an area for them, perhaps providing them in advance with special stickers so that parking marshals recognise these vehicles when they arrive.

Liaison with course planner(s) over start and finish locations is also vital. If, as is hoped, it is possible to integrate the start and the finish, it is essential that wheelchair competitors can get to and from them. An extra lane wide enough to allow wheelchair competitors through without difficulty is recommended for both start and finish. At a major event this is most likely to be near the colour-coded or string course start and finish.

First aid

First aid is usually provided at orienteering events, and any group offering this service should be informed that disabled athletes will be taking part and may need access.

Toilets

Toilet facilities for disabled competitors allowing wheelchair access should be provided. Additionally, the nearest accessible public toilets should be detailed in the pre-event information.

Toilets suitable for people with disabilities can be hired from most companies providing a service for outdoor events. An alternative source of help in Britain is the local social services department, or organisations such as the Red Cross who loan a frame which can be placed over a chemical toilet housed in a large frame tent.

Marshals

A point worth repeating is that on Trail O courses, competitors may receive physical assistance at any stage, but no help with decision-making. It may be necessary to provide extra helpers on steep or rough sections of the route.

Unfortunately, it must be recognised that with control markers and signs all beside paths, or within 60 metres in the terrain, the equipment is vulnerable, and may be damaged or removed by those who find it amusing to spoil other people's enjoyment. However, constant patrolling is relatively easy with a number of marshals circulating throughout the time that controls are in position. These marshals should not establish a circuit but move at random and separately. In some areas radio phones would be an asset. If allowed in the area, mountain bikes may be a valuable aid in covering the ground effectively. Extra protection can be supplied by the marshals working at the timed controls and those offering extra physical assistance along the route.

Punching

On all courses, having made their decision, competitors may mark or punch their card out of sight of other competitors, but before arriving at the next control site. In top competitions organisers may supply competitors with up to 3 sticky labels. These may be used to correct punching mistakes before leaving a decision area. Marshals may inspect the card at any point along the route to monitor punching. In some competitions these marshals may have a results template and can indicate verbally how competitors are faring; some may not wish to know. Some form of control, by joining all punched boxes with a line, by endorsing the card or possibly endorsing any corrected box, would be required, and competitors would not be allowed to retrace their route on learning of any error.

Control Card

A control card to be photocopied onto appropriately coloured paper appears as Appendix C. Trim off the boxes on the right leaving boxes A-C only for courses N, C and B. Supply two joined at the short edges by clear sticky tape, protected by a polythene bag.

Don't judge the control site from a standing position.
Take a stool to see how it looks to the disabled person.
Assess the suitability of the path by taking the equipment round first in a shopping trolley

Drawings: Guthrie Hutton

Planning Trail O Courses

The aim is to provide an enjoyable experience in the countryside while adding a mental challenge, but not to overtax the physical ability of the competitors. Where possible, courses should include controls placed for their scenic value as well as for their navigational challenge.

When planning, use a stool to check visability at each control site. When first checking sites try wheeling the required equipment in a shopping trolley or pushchair, as it will give an indication of how navigable the route is.

Because levels of disability will be variable among competitors, it is essential to predraw or overprint all maps; accuracy is of paramount importance. Except for novices, the IOF descriptions should be the norm. The concepts in planning for Trail O vary considerably from other course planning as the sites are only viewable from one side, that of the path, or occasionally an accessible area just off the path. The correct site, shown on the competitor's map by the centre of the control circle and described on the control description sheet, will be identified in the terrain by a control marker; this feature must have been correctly interpreted by the mapper. False control sites nearby will be identified in the terrain by identical control markers. For the easier courses these will be on distinctly different

Drawing: Guthrie Hutton

features, but for more experienced competitors they may be on similar or even identical features which may be too indistinct or small to be shown on the map.

For example on course A, for control number 3 the circle on the map is drawn showing the feature as a boulder; the description for A3 will be 'boulder'. From the map it is clear that only boulders over 1.5m have been shown; on site there is a group of four boulders, each with a control marker as shown. However, when viewing from position 'X', the competitor will know that the marker to the left is named A and that on the right D, and will therefore punch his or her card in box A3-B. Position 'X' on the pathside will be shown by a coded stake, eg 'A3'.

It is important, particularly as the intention is to integrate Trail O within mainstream orienteering, to identify and diffentiate the markers used on Trail O courses. It is suggested that the TR logo is used. The logo could be mounted as a card and fixed to the stake above the marker.

In view of the number of false controls, the planner will need a substantial number of markers, and this will obviously mean more time setting out the course than usual. This should be a team effort, with the planner or controller sitting on a stool on the path at the control identification stake, and assistants (one per marker) placing the markers on predetermined, identically taped sites. (Controls are usually pre-marked and these tapes are not removed. The competitors may spot the tapes. If the 'real' site is marked with a different coloured tape from the false controls, the whole game will be given away.)

To enable competitors to get a 'feel' for the ground shape, control markers should be hung, as far as possible, at a standard height. It is suggested that the bottom edge of the marker should be 50cm above ground level. Vegetation around the site may need restraining or even clearing, though it is acceptable for only part of the marker to be visible from the relevant path viewing point.

Ambulant competitors may need to bend or even be offered a seat, especially at timed controls.

Courses

The suggested distance for a control site appropriate to each course is given below, however common sense should prevail and in open areas where there is uninterrupted visibility of 200m or more distances can be lengthened. Equally in areas of very thick vegetation, they must be reduced.

The start of any route not physically passable by a wheelchair must be taped across at the junction with the main route. Genuine route choice is to be encouraged, however.

Novice (N) Courses

Courses planned for this class should be technically easy (at level 1) with all the control sites on, or no more than 5m from, the paths at junctions or where other distinct features abutt the path on which competitors are travelling. In suitable areas Trail O courses can be linked with other novice courses. (See also chapter 4)

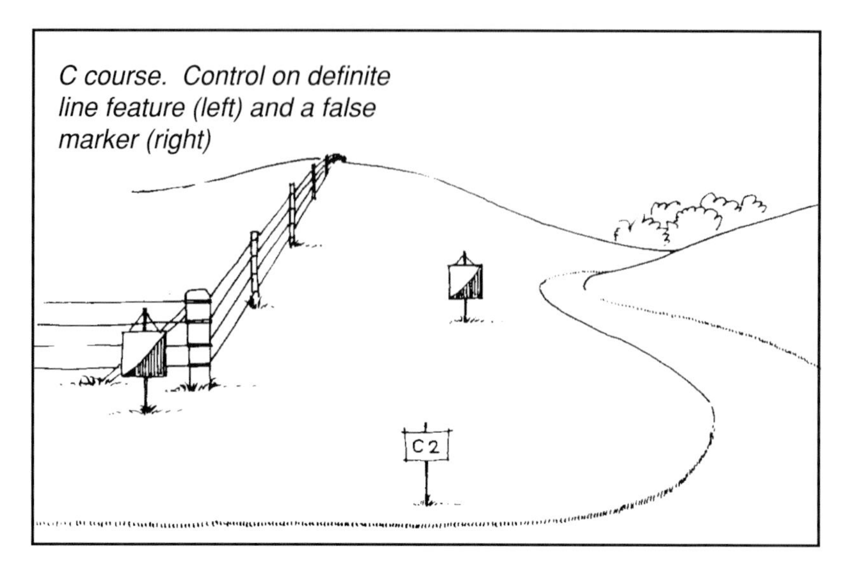

C course. Control on definite line feature (left) and a false marker (right)

Drawing: Guthrie Hutton

C Courses
The C course should be of technical level 2 in difficulty. Control sites will be on or within 10m of the path on which competitors are travelling. Line or other distinct features will be used as control sites and a false control marker may be placed at each site, but not too close to the correct marker and on a distinctly different feature. The false marker may also be placed anywhere (i.e. on no definite feature at all). The course should be from 1.0km - 2.0km in length with up to ten controls.

B Courses
The B course should be of technical level 3, 1.5km - 2.5km in length and have up to 15 controls. Control sites may be up to 20m from the path or track, but must be clearly visible from the marked viewing point. Up to two false controls may be hung in the vicinity of the control marker on different (or similar, but not identical features unless the false one is clearly outside the control circle).

When the area allows, simple route choices may be incorporated, together with the use of easily navigable areas off the main track. The fact that competitors may have to retrace their routes (dog-leg) is not considered a fault, and such deviation from the main path can add to the quality of the course.

Very obvious contour features may be used on this course for some, but not all of the control sites. The viewing position will be marked at the pathside. There will need to be at least one timed control.

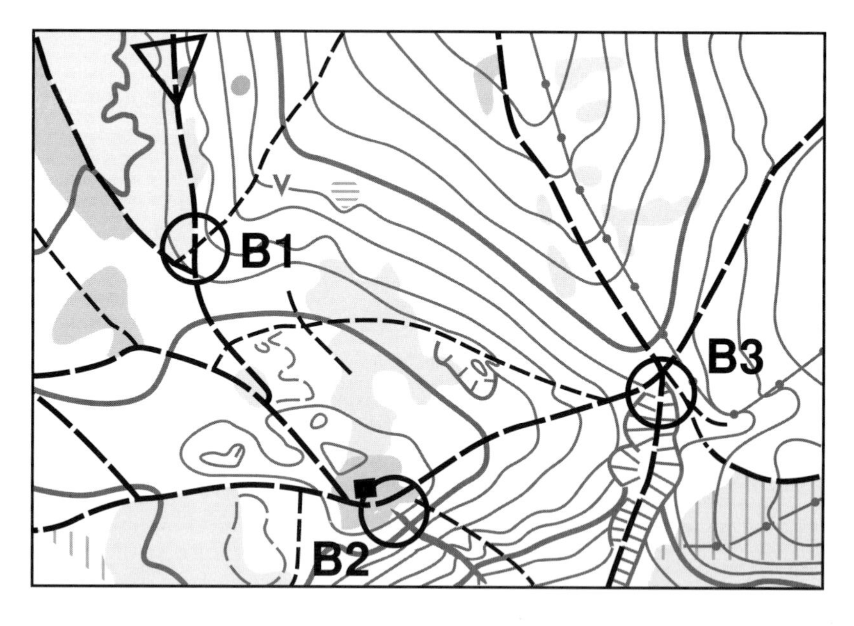

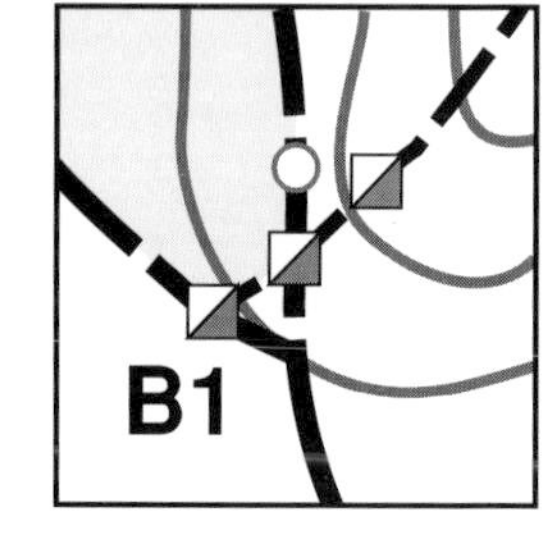

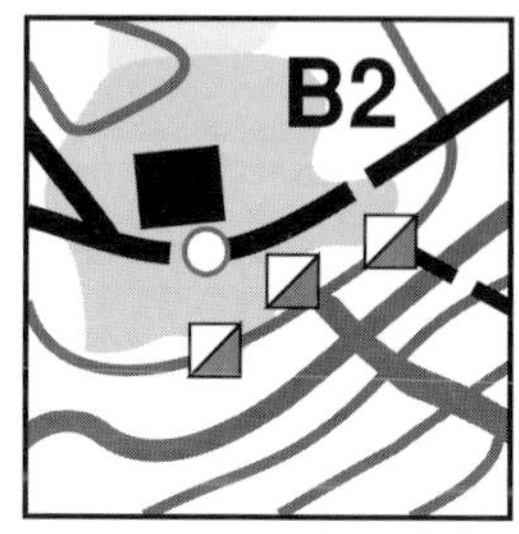

B course controls. Upper map at 1:5000, lower maps enlarged to show viewing point and location of markers

A Courses

The A course should be of technical level 5, from 1.5km - 3.0km in length, with up to 20 controls, which may be hung up to 40m from the indicated viewing point. This course should be as varied as possible and competitors can be expected to negotiate, with physical assistance if required, small paths and reasonable gradients.

If at all possible, some route choice should be provided between control sites, and many dog-legs off the main track. Small features requiring a good understanding of contour lines and variations in vegetation will provide suitable control sites.

There will be up to three false controls at each site. These can be hung on similar features to the correct site; indeed, this is desirable, and provides an even greater challenge if, because of the map scale the smaller examples of that feature are not shown on the map. There should be two or even three timed controls

A course controls. Map left at 1:5000, maps right enlarged to show viewing point and location of markers

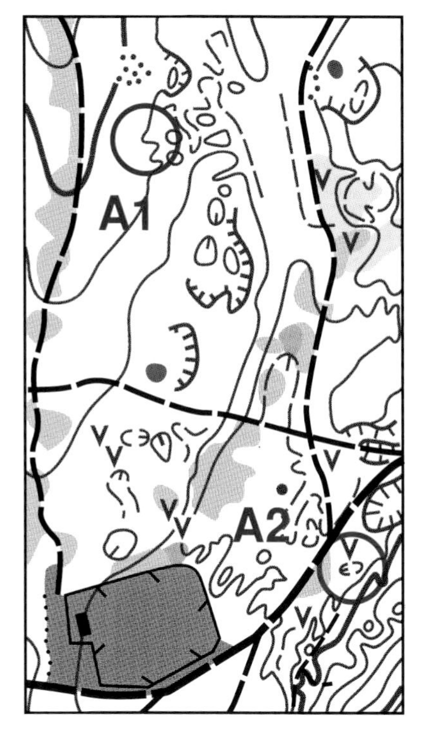

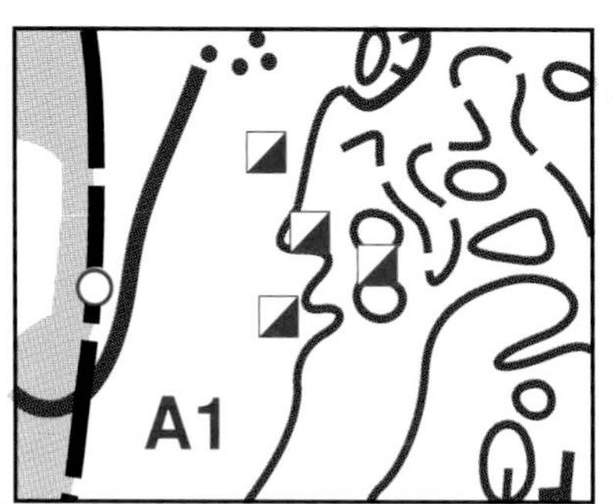

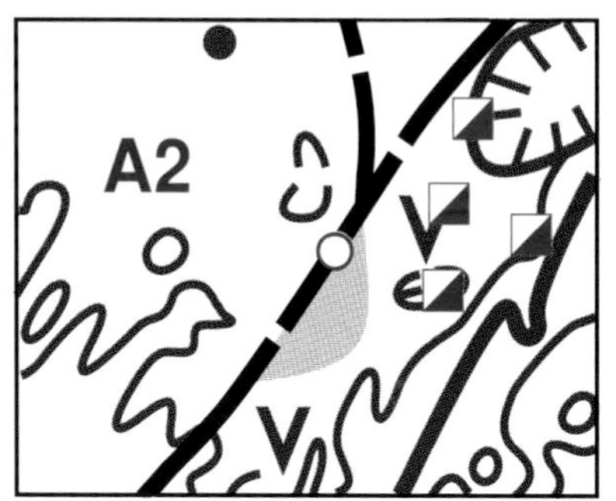

Elite (E) Courses

For the elite and experienced Trail O competitor, the E course will be as difficult as possible. The course will be 2.0km - 3.5km in length with up to 25 controls, which can be hung 60m or more from the main path. Remember all control markers must be at least partly visible when sitting.

E course controls. Map left at 1:5000, map right enlarged to show location of markers (no viewing point)

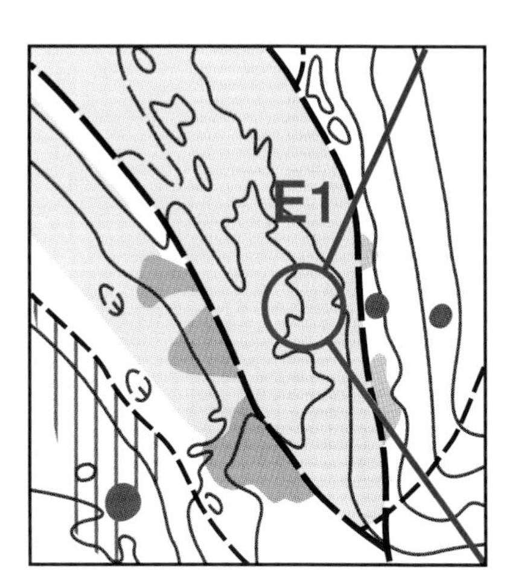

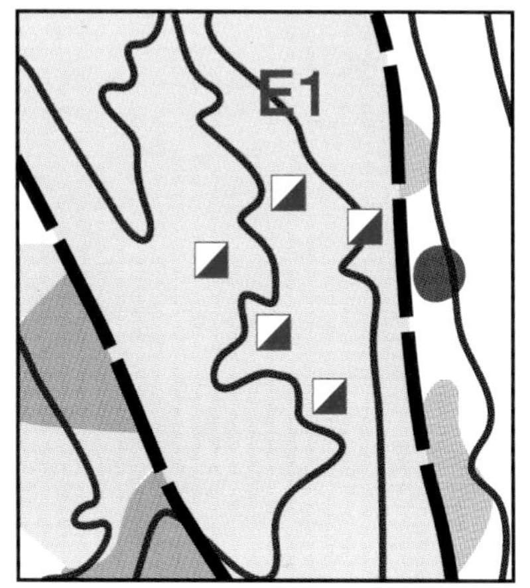

The same group of control markers may be used for A & E courses, normally with a different control description and therefore, most likely, a different correct answer. At least some of the control sites should be different. Only the E course can have the situation where none of the markers represents the centre of the control circle and description. Timed controls as for the A courses.

Visibility from a wheelchair is very important, and it may be possible to improve this by tying back or some pruning of lower branches of trees near the path.

The overprint can be used to show impassable routes. The IOF (X) symbol would be used. If, for example, none of the small paths on a particular map is negotiable by a wheelchair, possibly an overprint in the legend is the best way to show this.

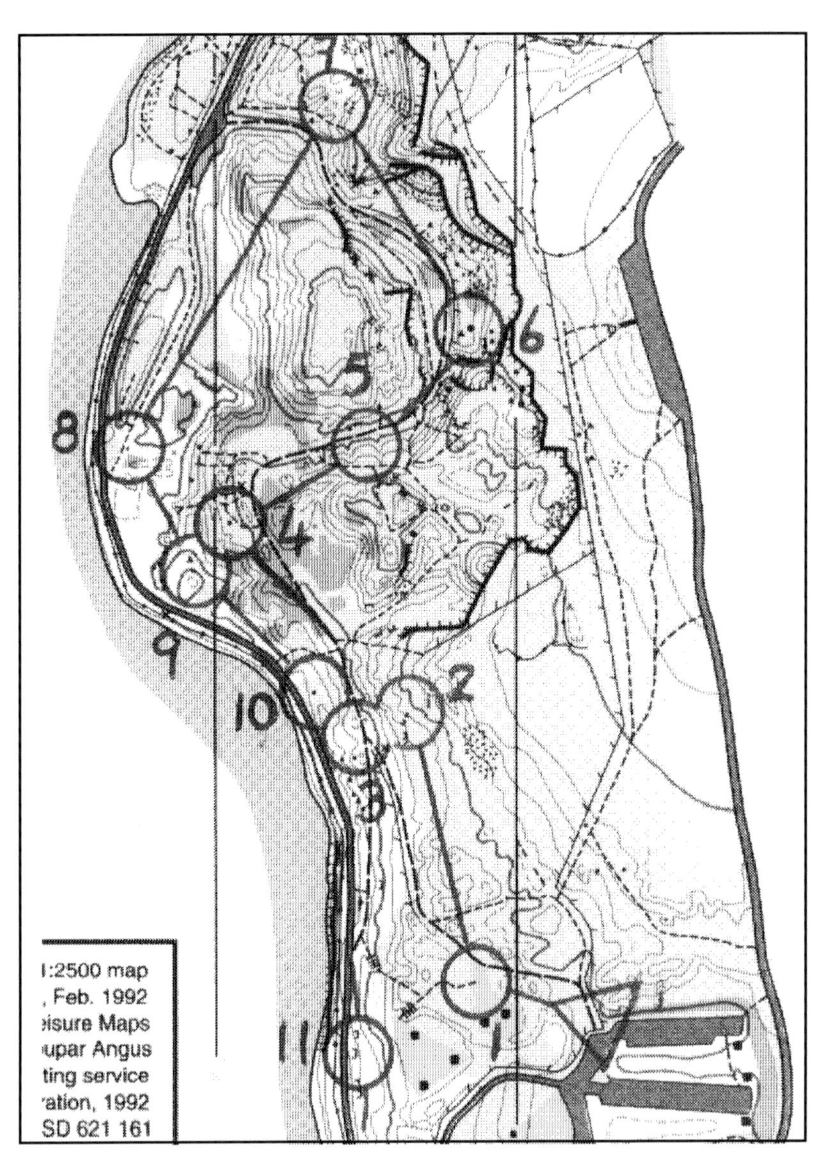

Timed controls

Timed controls are preferably placed in an area where they can only be seen by those competitors actually at the control, and also where no-one can work out the location in advance. Logistically, it is useful to start the competition with the timed control(s) and issue the individual competition maps <u>after</u> that stage.

Two marshals must be at the site, the first to position the competitor and get him or her ready, the second to operate the watch and record the result. If the timed control(s) is partway round the course, further marshals are needed to stop competitors and collect their maps. These can be stapled in an envelope so that the competitor can carry the map to the next marshal for return after completing the time control procedure. The time the competitor arrives at this marshall must be recorded, as should any time spent waiting to proceed towards the timed control. The results team must have this information so that no competitor incurs penalty points as a result of organisational holdups.

It is considered inappropriate to have the timed control at the end of the course as this gives competitors an opportunity to predetermine the likely site, and offers the possibility of studying the map detail in advance.

Competitor	Answer	Time taken	Score	Time recorded
1	correct	21 sec	1	0m 21 sec
2	wrong	6 sec	0	1m 06 sec
3	correct	1m 56 sec	1	1m 56 sec
4	wrong	1m 50 sec	0	2m 50 sec
5	none	2m	0	3m

Time allowance

There should be a maximum time allowance for competitors to complete their course (a logistic aid for the organiser). This is worked out by the planner and should be the time taken to complete the distance in an unassisted wheelchair, plus an allowance for each control on the longest course. Any delay caused by the race organisation, a queue at a timed control for instance, must be recorded and the elapsed time deducted from the competition time. The only reason for recording start and finish times is to check that the maximum course time allowance has not been exceeded; if it has, to discourage undue delay on the course, the competitor has one point deducted for every 5 minutes, or part of 5 minutes, in excess of the maximum time.

Results

When checking results, any line on a card with more than one punchmark must be discounted by drawing a line through it prior to counting the correctly punched boxes. An easy way to check cards is to make a template from a control card with windows which reveal the boxes that should contain punchmarks. This is then fitted over the competitor's card, and the correct answers can be counted and recorded. A correctly punched card should be displayed in the finish area.

For Trail O courses, the results display should be placed at suitable heights for those confined to wheelchairs and those standing, and should be printed to be large enough to be read from two metres away.

The results display should include copies of the competition map showing the control circles and the location of the false controls for each course. It could also show the viewing point. This would be particularly valuable for E course competitions. A black and white photocopy is the easiest way to make an enlarged version of this master map.

Although all competitors on a course will participate on equal terms, the results should differentiate between competitors restricted by any form of disability (as declared at registration) and those in an open class. The two sets of results should be presented alongside each other - perhaps offset on the sheet - for easy comparison.

With multi-day competitions, the final results are obtained by adding together the points gained on each day and the total time taken for all timed controls; the winner being the competitor with the highest score and lowest elapsed time.

Sample results list
Course A Fawn 3km, 20 controls (2 timed)

	Restricted		Open	
1 Joan Phillips			16	0m 23sec
2. Bruce Brown			16	0m 44sec
3. Kenneth Petters	14	1m 09sec		
4. Brigit Johnson	14	1m 13sec		
5. Colin Allen			14	1m24sec
6. Tom Ericson	12	1m 17sec		
7. Michael Applewhite	12	1m 22sec		
8. Sue Harrington	11	1m 02sec		
9. Dave Gerrard	11	1m 03sec		

Trail Orienteering Technical Guidelines

Class	**N**	**C**	**B**	**A**	**E**
Colour	**CREAM**	**ROSE**	**SKY**	**FAWN**	**GREY**
Terrain	Easy. Not steep. No very small paths. Open areas/ buildings are used	As N	More forest terrain. There can be gradients. Small paths can be used	Mostly forest terrain. Hills can be used. Small paths used a lot.	As A
Map	Not too many details, no use of contour lines necessary	As N	Varied maps - more details in parts of course. Contours can be used but not excessively.	As varied as possible. Contour lines are very important	As A
Degree of difficulty	From 0-2 junctions. No route choice. Few changes of direction. No crossovers	As N	Simple route choice. Variety of lengths of legs. Many changes of direction possible. 'Dog legs' used. Crossovers avoided.	Complicated route choice to control points. Big variation in paths used. Many 'dog legs'	As A
Use of compass example	To orientate map only	N-S, E-W only	1 compass problem, E one of group or N side of feature	2 or more N. eastern of group on S side	As many as N western of group on S western side looking from east
Control points	Very easy on or close to line. Precise control descriptions	As N	Line features and point features (large). Not too complicated description	Small features. Knowl-edge of contour lines. Very difficult descriptions.	As A Small and more diffuse details if possible
False control	None	Very different feature	Not on similar features	Parallel/similar features desirable, false sites not necessarily on map	As A All markers may be on false sites
No. of markers at site	1	2	3	4	5
Attack Point	Only distant line features	As N	Line features. Some crags/ boulders that are obvious, as with contour features	As small and diffuse as possible. Contour lines used.	As A Can be further distance from control
Viewing Point	Yes (+ punch)	Yes	Yes	Yes	No
Length	1.0 - 2.0km	As N	1.5 - 2.5km	1.5 - 3.0km	1.5 - 3.5km
No. of control points	8 - 10	10-12	12-15	15-20	15-25
Distance from path to control site	0 - 5m	0 - 10m	0 - 20m	0 - 40m	0 - 40m+
Timed controls	No	No	1 (2?)	min. 1	min. 2

Part 2

Chapter 12 For Mappers

Given suitable terrain, it is quite possible to use existing maps for Trail Orienteering. Methods of adapting existing maps are considered later in this chapter.

However, as Trail O becomes an integrated part of the sport, it is desirable for mappers to be made aware before surveying begins of the problems disabled competitors might face in the area being used. It is therefore important to note any obstacles which might restrict wheelchair-bound orienteers, such as gates, narrow footbridges, steps and steep gradients, as well as paths and tracks with poor surfaces. Mappers should also be aware of how improved map legibility can help competitors with impaired vision or learning difficulties.

Special Obstacles

A wide variety of normally unmapped features on an orienteering map can constitute impassable obstacles for the wheelchair-bound competitor. In order to provide a safe, fair course, the mapper needs to find some way to introduce these - by the use of special symbols where necessary - on to the map. Except in relatively rare circumstances, it is not considered likely that maps will be produced specifically for disabled competitors. The solution is to adopt a system which can easily show obstacles on a course overprint.

Surveying

When surveying for Trail O it is important to remember that the competitor will only view the control sites from the path, and it is the view from this aspect that is therefore important. It should be drawn as seen from a sitting position. Much attention must be given to the area near the tracks and paths and up to 100m from these routes.

Detail very close to paths is sometimes shown inconsistently on o-maps - mounds of earth, boulders thrown up by road building, small thickets, etc. If a map might be used for Trail O, more care should be taken to make sure that this detail is correct - what is visible from a path or track is clear on the map. There will be detail which is obvious from a path but might not be significant when taken in the context of the map as a whole. In this situation it might be worthwhile for the surveyor to record a category of detail that would only appear on the Trail O edition of a map. With computerised map drawing this would present little problem (see later section).

The position of steps must be noted as anything other than very shallow ones, more than 1.5m apart, make the route impassable for a wheelchair, and therefore any Trail O competitor. It is suggested that horizontal lines across the path be used to show steps, and if they are impassable they should have a cross superimposed.

It is common practice for cartographers to exaggerate the distance of a knoll, or other point feature, from a line feature as a way of presenting a clear picture. This is not normally a problem. However in Trail O the relationship of all features is critical and the interpretation of the map vital. It therefore matters whether the knoll is shown as being 1m, 5m or 10m from the path, especially as there may also be other smaller knolls in the vicinity which will not be mapped but are clear in the terrain.

The existing path/track/road symbols could be adapted to indicate their suitability for wheelchairs. If a small bar were added to every dash of a path or track, this could indicate that the route is impassable to a wheelchair. For a specifically impassable feature, the overprinted cross as detailed in the IOF specification should be used. Details of the symbols and their classification can be found in the booklet *International Specifications for Orienteering Maps.*

Additional control sites can be created for Trail O by careful representation of vegetation boundaries. In an area covered in boulders only boulders of sufficient size will be shown. Similarly, in woodland, any extra large trees, say with a trunk greater than 0.75m diameter, could be shown, as should any tree that is significant, either in woodland or open land. This is a category of detail that is suitable as an addition to the standard o-map when it will be used for Trail O. This map may be a separate print run or the Trail O detail could be added as an overprint to the standard map. With computerised maps a limited run of colour copies is simple.

If special or adapted symbols are used, information such as 'surface suitable for a wheelchair' and 'surface unsuitable for a wheelchair' should be inserted in the key where appropriate.

Legibility

Much attention has been given to this in recent years in relation to vision problems affecting older able-bodied competitors (far-sightedness). The recommended solution has been to increase all line thicknesses on 1:10,000 maps by 50% compared to 1:15,000 symbol dimensions. This is achieved by either (a) drawing the 1:10,000 artwork with thicker lines, or (b) photo-enlarging existing maps to increase both scale and line thicknesses.

Park map with extra information added for Trail O. 1:5,000

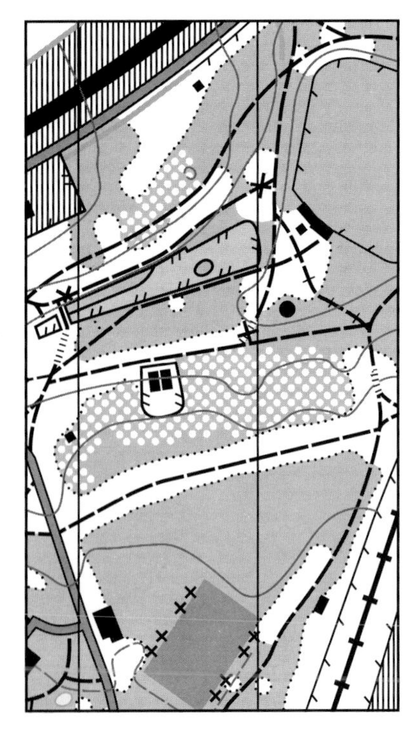

Selecting a scale

1:15,000. This is the standard competition o-map scale and the least suitable for Trail O, having relatively fine line thickness and small symbol size. Where new maps are being produced, it would be helpful to look at the feasibility of photo-enlarging all or part of the map to 1:10,000. If you are considering this, it is wise to contact one of the professional mapping companies for advice before you begin drawing the map, particularly if you are enlarging only part of the map.

1:10,000. Many existing British maps are drawn to this scale, using the line/symbol specifications 50% larger than those for 1:15,000 maps - in other words the map is drawn as if it is a photo-enlargement from a 1:15,000 map. When surveying for 1:10,000 maps, it is important that the larger scale is not used to incorporate unnecessary detail which would adversely affect legibility.

Larger scales. Maps at 1:5,000 and 1:2,500 are often used for very small areas or for instructing beginners. BOF have produced a booklet giving advice on how to draw maps for permanent courses which contains suggestions for symbol/line sizes for very large scale maps in both black and white and colour. In general, line thicknesses should be as per 1:10,000 maps above. Point symbols such as boulders, dot knolls etc often look rather lost at very large scales, and it is suggested that they should be drawn at twice the 1:15,000 size. There are many instances where increasing all line dimensions by 200% is the best solution.

Computers in map drawing

The majority of new maps that are produced today are drawn on a computer. Most commonly this is either on a PC using a programme written specifically for orienteering called O-CAD, or on an Apple Macintosh using a programme such as Illustrator. This development has great potential for special versions of standard orienteering maps, particularly if a small number of copies is required. It is possible to have an additional layer of detail that can be turned on or off. It is then easy to print out just a small section of a map - at any scale. Colour copies can be printed directly. High quality colour copying is now possible with copiers that have a processor to interface directly from the computer disk - such as the Canon 500 or bubblejet printer. The cost is not high.

Using existing maps

However the orienteering map is produced, additional information will be needed on existing maps to help the disabled orienteer. The easiest (and cheapest) way to achieve this is to incorporate such information with the course overprint in red or purple. To keep the maps as simple and legible as possible, the minimum number of new symbols should be used.

For wheelchair competitors, a single symbol indicating an impassable route or obstacle can be used. The existing IOF symbol for a forbidden route (X) is suggested; this has the added advantage of being present in most hand-operated overprinting kits. Where the obstacle is small (e.g. a stile or flight of steps), one cross can be used. For impassable sections of path or terrain, a row of crosses or bars across the path dashes should be used.

Information

The following publications may be found useful.

- International Specifications for Orienteering Maps (IOF).
- Mapmaking for Orienteers by Robin Harvey (Harveys).
- Drawing Maps for Permanent Courses by Peter Roberts & Chris Shaw (BOF).

All these are available through Harveys or the British Orienteering Federation National Office (addresses on p64).

Part 2

Chapter 13 Types of Disability and Disability Awareness

The disabled should not be considered en masse. Firstly, their interests are as diverse as those of the able-bodied population; and secondly, the range of disabilities and the different problems created by them affect each person in a quite specific and individual way.

Disability has been defined as any restriction or lack of ability (resulting from an impairment) to perform an activity in the manner or within the range considered normal for a human being. The disabled therefore have a wide range of abilities and, for some, little or no modification to normal orienteering events or courses is needed.

Disabled people have the same needs, hopes, emotions, enthusiasms and involvements as anybody. It follows that their reasons for participating in sport are the same as everyone else's - but it may be that satisfaction (at achievement) and frustration (at non-achievement) are somewhat greater. Many have hidden and untapped talents. They neither expect nor wish to have everything done for them and want to be involved in decision making.

It is easy to fall into the trap of worrying about someone's disability rather than focussing on getting to know them as a person. The key is to find out what can be done rather than what cannot.

How to communicate

Before doing anything - ask. Talk with whoever you are helping to find out what is required of you.

The best tutor is usually the disabled person, but do find out how much they know about the job in hand as well.

It is important to set up a two-way dialogue so as to break down preconceived ideas and build confidence on both sides. This will also clarify the general area of the disability - physical/sensory/ learning or, more rarely, combinations of the three.

If communication is difficult due to the disability there will almost certainly be an escort present from whom you can obtain more information.

Helping is a very personal matter, so always aim to build trust. This may take time but will enable both parties to function eventually as a team. Try not to take over; carry on with your two-way conversation to find out more about strengths and limitations, then help accordingly.

You may encounter a variety of problems associated with disability. All can, and indeed are, dealt with on a daily basis. Some things to bear in mind are paralysis, balance, co-ordination, pain, lack of feeling, temperature control, poor communication, endurance levels, limitation of joint movement, lack of sight/hearing, going to the loo, etc. Don't worry. There is always someone around to help - find out who they are and make yourself know to them.

For disabled people and helpers alike the two ground rules are:

- the right to say "No, I can't do that", and
- never patronise.

Historically, sport for the disabled has been organised according to seven categories of disability; visual handicap, deafness, mental handicap, paraplegia/tetraplegia, cerebral palsy, limb amputation and 'les autres'. Trail orienteering will not differentiate between disabilities, which may even be temporary.

Visual handicap
Visual impairment includes both total blindness and various forms of partial sight - short sightedness, age-related failing eyesight, and a variety of field of vision restrictions such as tunnel vision. For people with severe visual impairment, mainstream orienteering is likely to be inappropriate. For those with minor visual impairment, magnifiers are available. Large scale uncluttered maps, usually enlarged from 1.15,000 maps, are beneficial.

Trail O with large scale maps may be more appropriate than timed courses and may provide a better introduction for newcomers.

Deafness
Auditory impairment includes total deafness and a broad range of levels of partial hearing, including those who are born deaf and have communication problems. Hearing impairment is not usually a major problem to orienteers, though start officials should be prepared to signal to deaf competitors where a whistle is in use.

Learning difficulty (mental handicap)
This term is used to describe the wide-ranging conditions experienced by those with intellectual impairments. People with mental handicaps form the largest single group of disabled people in the community, and are bound to be well represented at events that are advertised to 'the disabled'.

At mainstream events, no special provision is usually needed other than advice as to the colour-coding that is most appropriate. Those with more severe learning difficulties will require a higher level of preparation and teaching and are likely to find a 'string' course the most suitable first experience. It would be sensible to allow mentally handicapped orienteers to compete in pairs, or to run with a 'buddy'.

Paraplegia/tetraplegia
Paraplegia refers to paralysis of both legs, which may be caused by injury to the spinal cord or by disease. The degree of paralysis depends on the site of the lesion. If it is in the lower back, the person may be able to walk with the aid of calipers and/or crutches. If it is in the chest or thoracic section, the person may lose the use of part of or all of the hands and arms as well, a condition known as tetraplegia.

In the main, people with spinal cord-linked disabilities will be wheelchair participants. These will provide the greatest challenge to course planners and organisers.

Trail orienteering is a sport that uses the brain and is therefore available to those with severe physical disabilities unable to enjoy undue exertion. It is therefore suitable to those who thought that sport was impossible.

Cerebral palsy
This term describes a group of non-progressive disorders in which brain damage before or at birth or during a child's early years causes impairment of motor function characterised by alteration of muscle tone and/or involuntary movement. Within cerebral palsy, people can have a wide range of differing abilities. Some may be able to take part in orienteering without modification, while others may be in wheelchairs.

Amputation
In sport, the term 'amputee' embraces those who have lost one or more limbs. Many amputees wear an artificial prosthesis which they may or may not wear to compete, others may be wheelchair bound but clearly amputees would be at a disadvantage on timed orienteering courses.

Les autres
This category meaning 'the others' covers a range of disabilities not included in the previous six categories, including congenital physical defects; many will enjoy Trail O.

Summary
Experience has shown that a significant number of disabled competitors have multiple handicaps, that those with learning difficulties generally outnumber the rest, and that the smallest group is that confined to wheelchairs. This latter group, while small in number, will find Trail Orienteering should be able to cater for their needs. It is particularly for them and others whose disability would place them at a disadvantage in traditional timed competition. That choice is of course always open.

Appendix A UK Organisations for the Disabled

British Sports Association for the Disabled (BSAD), Solecast House, 13/27 Brunswick Place, London N1 6DX. Tel: 071 490 4919.

BSAD has a mandate to:

• Provide opportuinities for people with any type of disability to enjoy and compete in physical recreation and sport in accordance with an individual's own wishes,

• Promote the benefits of physical recreation and sport to all people with disabilities and to encourage participation,

• Support clubs and local groups in their provision of recreational and sporting opportunities for people with disabilities and to help to introduce new sports,

• Educate the general public, the sporting world and the media to be aware of the sporting abilities and achievements of people with disabilities, in a step towards total interaction,

• Enhance the image and self-image of sport for people with disabili ties through a professional approach to the provision of sport,

• Encourage people with disabilities to take an active role in the organisation and development of sport at all levels.

BSAD produces a yearbook which includes much useful information.

Physically Handicapped - Able Bodied (PHAB), 12-14 London Road, Croydon, Surrey CR0 2TA. Tel: 081 667 9443.

Divisional Offices:	Scotland 031 229 3558
Northern Ireland 0232 370240	Wales 0222 488521
North of England 0423 505810	Midlands 021 440 4113
South West 0823 251004	South East 081 452 8020

PHAB is the only charity in the UK which exists solely to promote integration between physically disabled and able-bodied people. It is about realising ability and achieving real fulfilment for everybody. PHAB creates opportunities for people to come together on equal terms to break down the barriers of fear, ignorance and prejudice. PHAB has been involved from the outset in the formulation and development of Trail Orienteering in the UK.

UK Sports Association for People with Mental Handicaps, 30 Philip Lane, Tottenham, London N15 4JB.

British Paralympic Association, Room G13a, Delta Point, 35 Wellesley Road, Croydon, Surrey CR9 2YZ.

British Wheelchair Sports Foundation, Guttmann Sports Centre, Harvey Road, Stoke Mandeville, Bucks HP21 9PP.

Royal Association of Disability and Rehabilitation (RADAR), 25 Mortimer Street, London W1.

Scottish Sports Association for the Disabled, Fife Sports Institute, Viewfield Road, Glenrothes KY6 2RA (0592 771700).

The Sports Council, 16 Upper Woburn Place, London, WC1H 0QP (071 388 771700).

National Coaching Foundation, 4, College Close, Beckett Park, Leeds (0532 744802).

Appendix B Address List IOF Member Countries

* Associate Member

AUS	Orienteering Federation of Australia, PO Box 740, Glebe NSW 2037, Australia. Tel (61) 2 660 2067. Fax (61) 2 660 6661.
AUT	Osterreichischer Fachverband fuer OL, Prinz Eugenstr. 12, A-1040 Wien, Austria. Tel (43) 222 505 03 93. Fax (43) 222 505 08 45. Tlx. 133 132.
BEL	Association Belge de Sports d'Orientation, c/o Jean-Noel Debehogne, 31 avenue General Bernheim, B-1040 Bruxelles, Belgium. Tel (32) 2 640 6922.
BUL	Bulgarischer Touristenverband, OL-Foderation, Boul Tolbuchin Nr 18, Sofia 1000, Bulgaria. Tel 2 88 29 66, 52 10 02. Fax (359) 2 80 24 14.
CAN	Canadian Orienteering Federation, 1600 James Naismith Dr, Gloucester, Ontario KIB 5N4, Canada. Tel (1) 613 748 5649. Fax (1) 613 748 5706.
CHN	Chinese Orienteering Committee, No. 9 Tiyuguan Road, Beijing, China 100763. Tel (86) 1 75 13 13. Fax (86) 1 70 15 858.
CRO	Croatian Orienteering Federation, att.: Zeljko Gobec, Nova Ves 65, 41000 Zagreb, Croatia. Fax (38) 41 441 088.
CUB*	Angel Lenis Gual Salfran, President, Cuban Orienteering Federation, Via Blanca y Boyeros, INDER, Ciudad Deportiva Heipio Cerro, Zona Postal Habana 5, Cuba. Tel (53) 7 32 8441, 32 0636.
DEN	Dansk Orienterings-Forbund, Idraettens Hus, Brondby Stadion 20, DK-2605 Brondby, Denmark. Tel (45) 42 45 77 30, 42 45 55 55. Fax (45) 42 45 62 45 (please state: "Denmark Orienteering Federation"). Tlx. 33 111.
ESP	Agrupacion Espanola de Clubes de Orientacion (A.E.C.O.), Secretario General D. Eusebio Garcia Gomez, C/Concepcion 3, 2 G, E-28901 - Getafe (Madrid), Spain. Tel (34) 1-695 7965. Fax (34) 1-683 9652 (state: "fax").
EST	Eesti Orienteerumisliit, Regati 1, EE-0103 Tallinn, Estonia. Tel (7) 0142 23 70 21. Fax (7) 0142 23 83 55.
FIN	Suomen Suunnistusliitto, Radiokatu 12, SF-00240 Helsinki. Fax (358) 0 158 24 33. Tlx. 12 1797.
FRA	Federation Francaise de Course d'Orientation, B.P. 220. F-75967 Paris Cedex 20, France. Tel (33) 1 47 97 11 91. Fax (33) 1 47 97 90 29.
GBR	British Orienteering Federation, Riversdale, Dale Road North, Darley Dale, Matlock, Derbyshire DE4 2HX, England. Tel (44) 629 734 042. Fax (44) 629 733 769.
GER	Deutscher Turner Bund, Abteilung Sport, Otto-Fleck-Schneisse 8, W-6000 Frankfurt 71, Germany. Tel (49) 69 67 80 10. Fax (49) 69 67 80 11 79.
HKG	Orienteering Association of Hong Kong, Room 910, Queen Elizabeth Stadium, 18 Oi Kwan Road, Wan Chai, Hong Kong. Tel (852) 0 891 2691. Fax (852) 0 893 5654.
HUN	Magyar Tajekozodasi Futo, Szovetseg, Dozsa Gyorgy ut 1-3, H-1143 Budapest, Hungary. Tel (36) 1 113 64 88. Fax (36) 1 113 64 88. Tlx. 225 105.
IRL	Irish Orienteering Association, House of Sport, Longmile Road, Dublin 12, Ireland. Phone (353) 1 50 16 33. Fax (353) 1 50 28 05.

ISR Israel Sport Orienteering Association, Michael Friedlander, P.O. Box 1392, Ramat Hasharon 47 100, Israel. Tel (972) 3 49 01 65. Fax (972) 8 222 792.

ITA Federazione Italiana Sport Orientamento, Corso 3 Novembre 36, Cas. Post 640, I-38100 Trento, Italy. Tel (39) 461 916 900. Fax (30) 461 916 308.

JPN Nihon Orienteering Kyokai, Tsuruya bldg. 3F, Shiba 5-13-13, Mitato-ku, Tokyo, Japan 108. Phone (81) 3 5476 5657. Fax (81) 3 5476 5658.

KOR Korea Orienteering Federation, C.P.O. Box 3954, Seoul, Korea. Phone (82) 02 266 0140, 279 2941. Fax (82) 02 858 1193.

LAT Latvijas Orientesanas Federacija, 4 Terbatas Str., 226 723 Riga PDP, Latvia. Fax (7) 0132 28 44 12. Telex: 161183.

LIT Lietuvos Orientavimosi Sporto Federacija, Silo 5, 233 021 Kaunas, Lithuania. Tel (7) 0127 26 63 16. Fax (7) 0127 20 38 58.

MAS* Lee Kwan Meng, Committee for ASEAN Youth Co-operation, International Youth Centre, Jalan Tenteram, Bandar Tun Razak, Cheras, 56000 Kuala Lumpur, Malaysia. Fax (60) 3 971 6700.

NED Nederlands Orienteringsloop Bond, c/o Magreeth Vecht-Corts Leuvenumseweg 12, NL-3852 AS Ermelo, Netherlands. Tel 03417 59787.

NOR Norges Orienteringsforbund, Hauger Skolevei 1, N-1351 Rud, Norge. Tel (47) 2 87 46 00. Fax (47) 2 87 47 86. Tlx. 78 586 nif n.

NZL New Zealand Orienteering Federation, Chrissie Williams, PO Box 18836, New Brighton, Christchurch, New Zealand. Tel (64) 3 388 0798. Fax (64) 03 343 3354.

POL Polski Zwiazek Biegu na Orientacje, ul. Wilcza 38 a, 00-679 Warszawa, Poland. Tel (48) 22 29 50 04. Fax (48) 22 21 84 18. Tlx. 81 6407 cos pl.

POR Associacao Portuguesa de Orientacao, Av. Elias Garcia 177-2, P-1000 Lisboa, Portugal. Tel (351) 161 34 39. Fax (351) 793 3777.

ROM Romanian Orienteering Federation, 16, Vasile Conta Str., Sector 1, R-701 39 Bucharest, Romania. Tlx. 11180 sport r. Tel (40) 0 120 160. Fax (40) 0 120 161.

RSA Southern African Orienteering Federation, PO Box 90330, Bertsham 2013, South Africa. Tel (27) 11 680 8184. Fax (27) 11 806 4299.

RUS Orienteering Federation of Russia, ul. Furmanova, 12 119854 Moscow, Russia. Tel (7) 095 203 0776. Fax. (Pres.) (7) 8442 346 672.

SLO Orientacijska Zveza Slovenije, Brilejeva 1. 61000 Ljubljana, Slovenia. Tel & Fax. (38) 61 571 331.

SUI Schweizerischer Orientierungslauf-Verband, Marianne Bandixen, Gellerstrasse 43, CH-8222 Beringen, Schweiz. Tel (41) 53 35 16 15.

SVK Slovensky zvaz OB, Junacka 6, 83280 Bratislava, Slovakia. Tel (42) 7 214 362.

SWE Svenska Orienteringsforbundet, Idrottens Hus, S-123 87 Farsta, Sweden. Tel (46) 8 605 60 00. Fax (46) 8 605 63 60. Tlx. 141 79

TCH Cesky svaz orientacniho behu, Mezi stadiony, P.O.B. 40, 160 17 Praha 6 - Strahov, Ceska republika. Tel and fax (42) 2 354 679.

UKR Ukranian Orienteering Federation, OZOR, Boulevard Lepse, 55, 252065 Kiev, Ukraine. Fax. (7) 044 483 8032.

USA United States Orienteering Federation, P O Box 1444, Forest Park, GA 30051, USA. Tel. (1) 404 363 2110.

YUG YOF, Komisija za orijentaciju, Postanski Fah 33, YU-11420 Smederevska Palanka, Yugoslavia. Tel and fax (38) 26 33 031.

Appendix C International Control Description Symbols

Class	Course length in metres	Climbing in metres
H21E	12,300	270

A	B	C	D	E	F	G	H
5	49	(middle)	(boulder)		1.5	(north side)	(refreshments)

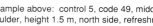

The most important items lie to the right of the thicker lines

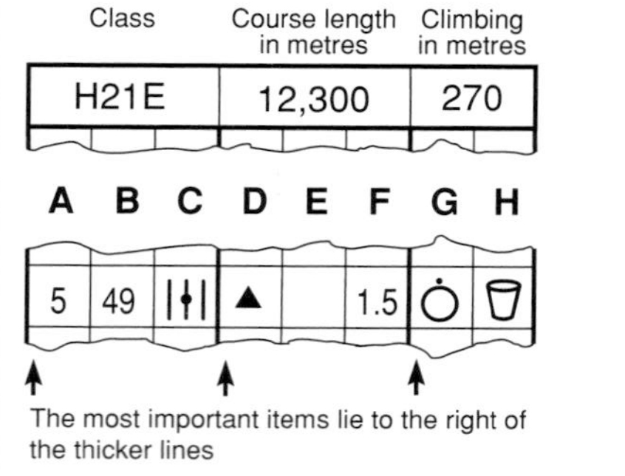

Example above: control 5, code 49, middle boulder, height 1.5 m, north side, refreshments

Key to Columns

A Control number
B Control code
C Which (of any similar) feature
D The control feature
E Details of appearance
F Dimensions of the feature
G Location of the marker
H Other information

Column C

- Southern
- Northeastern
- Upper
- Lower
- Middle

Column D

- Steep bank
- Quarry
- Earth bank, dam
- Terrace
- Spur
- Rib
- Re-entrant
- Gully
- Dry ditch
- Hill
- Knoll
- Saddle
- Depression
- Small depression
- Pit
- Cliff, crag
- Bare rock
- Cave
- Boulder
- Boulder field
- Stony ground
- Cairn/stone pile

Column D (cont.)

- Narrow passage (between cliffs)
- Lake
- Pond
- Waterhole
- Stream
- Ditch
- Marsh
- Small marsh
- Firm ground
- Well
- Spring
- Narrow marsh
- Seasonal watercourse
- Open land, field
- Semi-open land
- Forest corner
- Clearing
- Thicket
- Felled area
- Vegetation boundary
- Copse
- Hedge
- Linear thicket
- Road
- Path
- Narrow ride
- Wall
- Fence
- Footbridge

Column D (cont.)

- Building
- Ruin
- Tower
- Powerline
- Powerline pylon/pole
- Shooting platform
- Fodder rack
- Rock pillar
- Single tree
- Salt lick
- Root stock
- Boundary stone
- Charcoal burning ground
- Anthill
- Broken ground
- Special feature
- Special feature

Column E

- Shallow
- Deep
- Overgrown
- Open
- Rocky
- Marshy
- Sandy
- Coniferous
- Deciduous
- Ruined or collapsed

Column F

- 5.5 Height in metres
- 7x5 Size in metres
- 1.5/2.0 Height of object on a slope
- 1.5 2.0 Height of two objects in col. D

Column G

- North side
- Northwest edge
- East corner (inside)
- Southwest corner
- Southern tip
- Western part
- Upper part (head)

Column G (cont)

- Lower part (foot)
- On top of
- Southern foot
- Southwest end
- Between
- Bend
- At the foot (direction unspecified)

Column H

- Refreshments
- Radio control
- Manned control
- First aid

Combinations (D, E and F)

- Path crossing or intersection
- Path/ride crossing
- Road junction
- Stream/ditch junction

Marked routes

- 190 — 190m to finish, no tapes.
- 210 — 210m taped route away from control
- 50 — 50m taped route to map exchange
- 250 — 250m to finish, taped route
- 310 — 310m to finish, funnel tapes

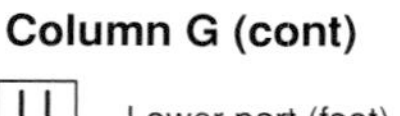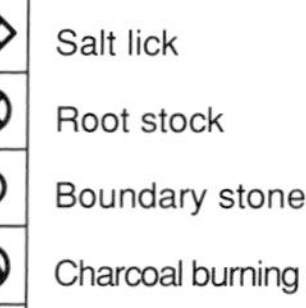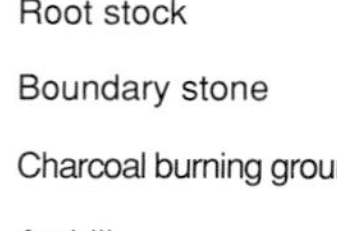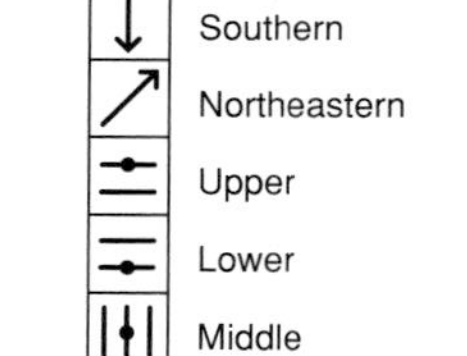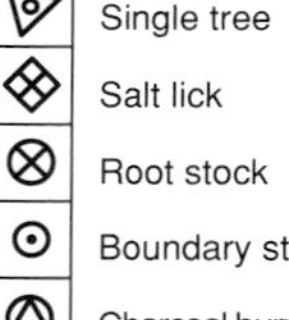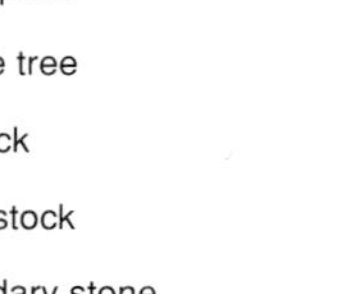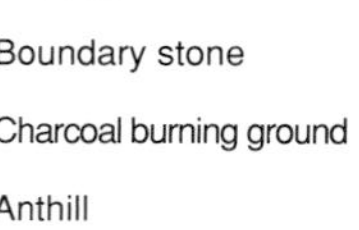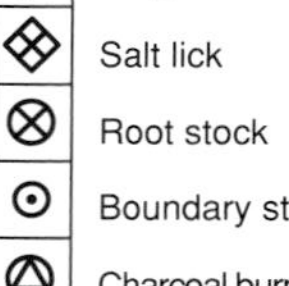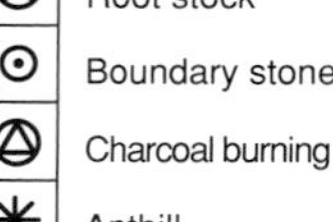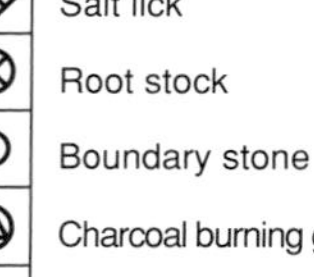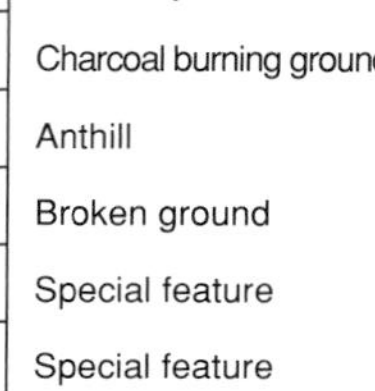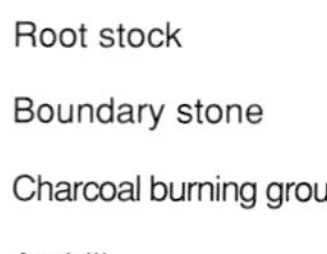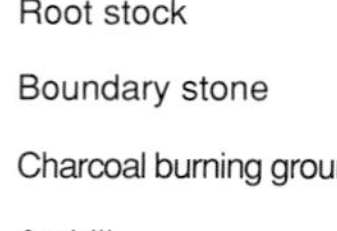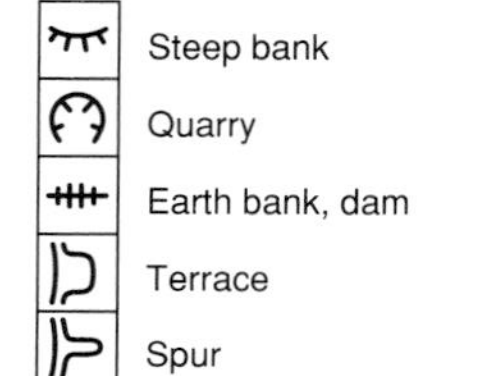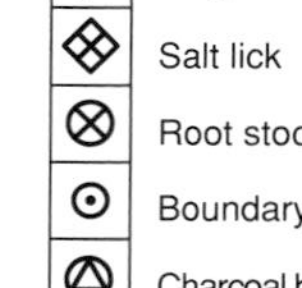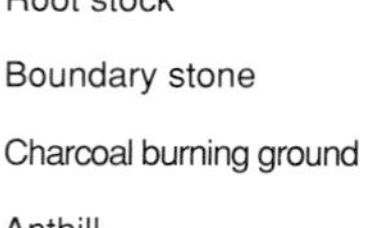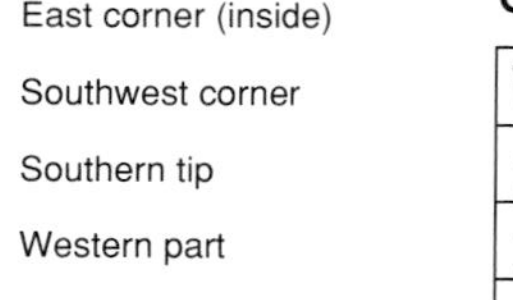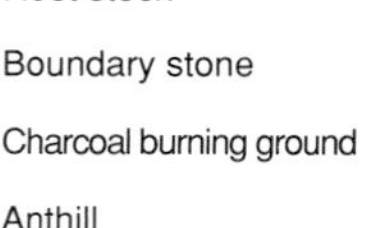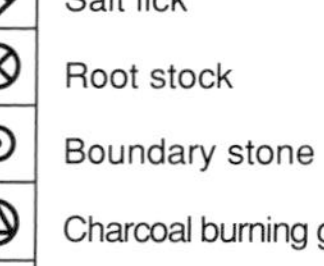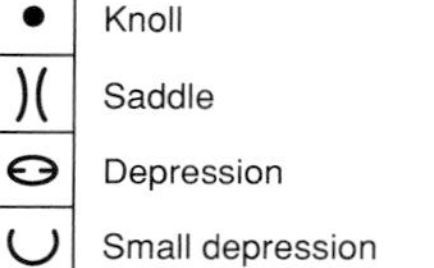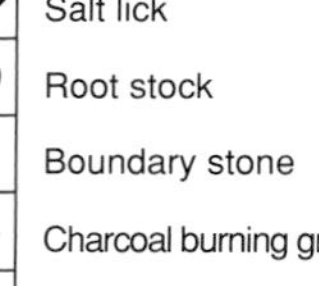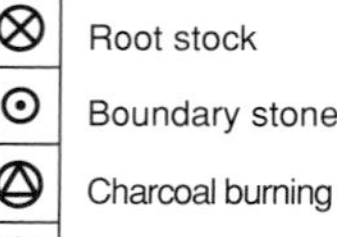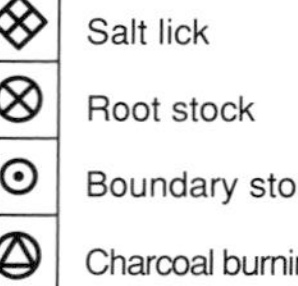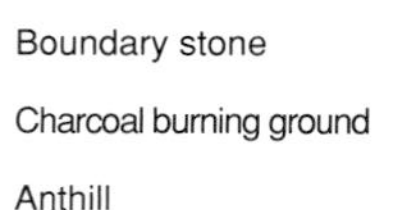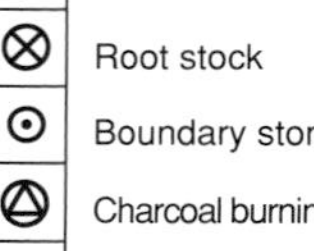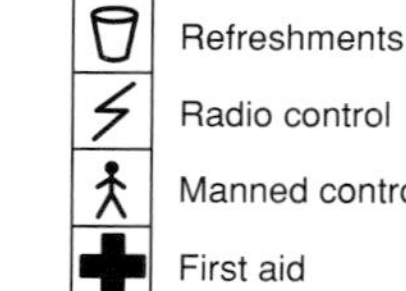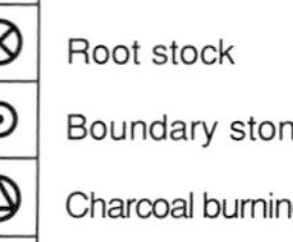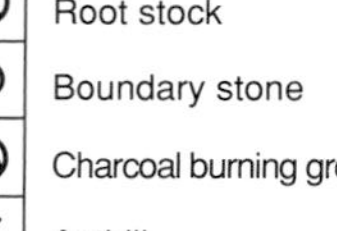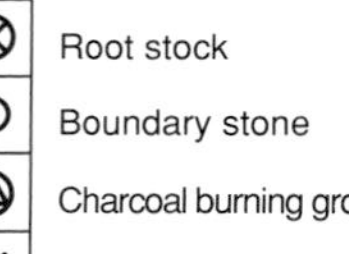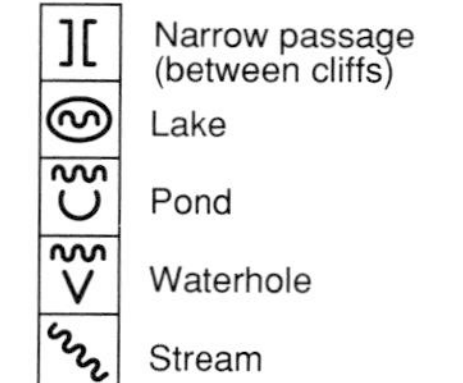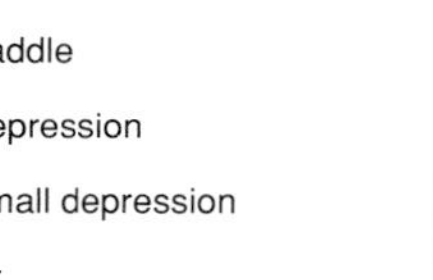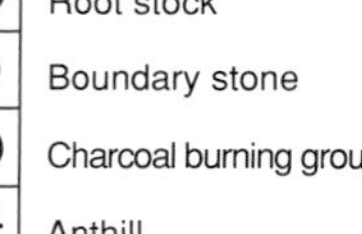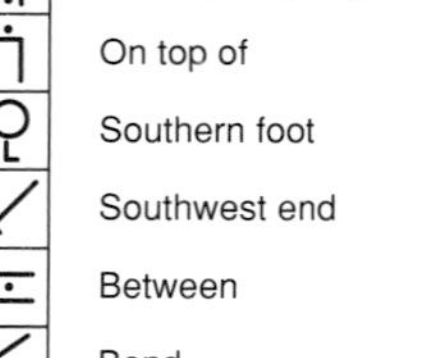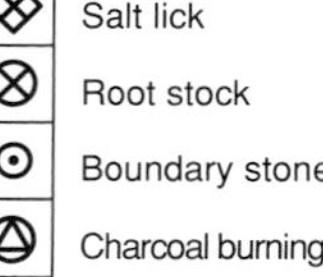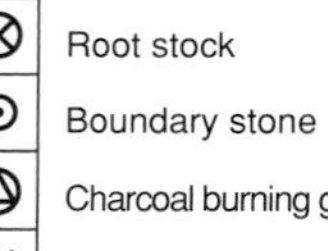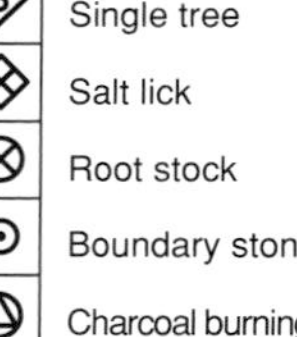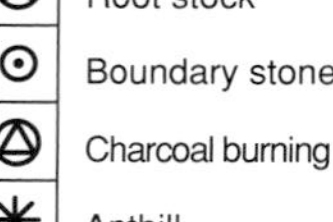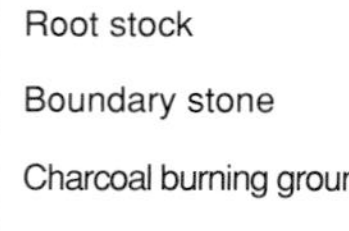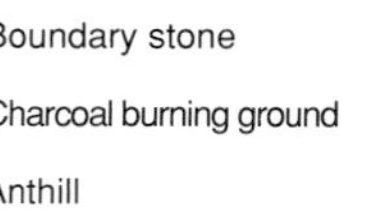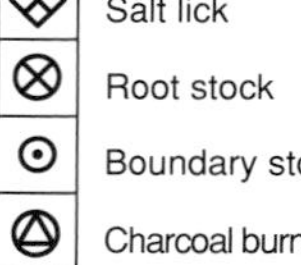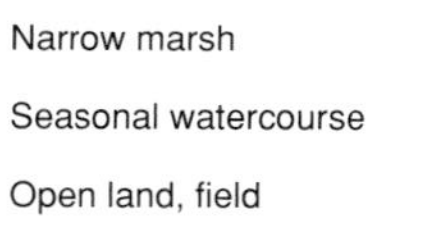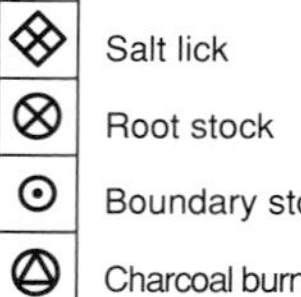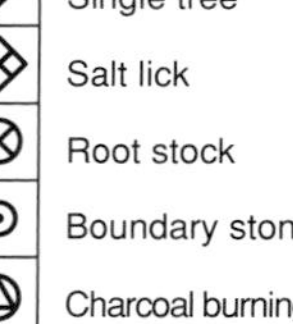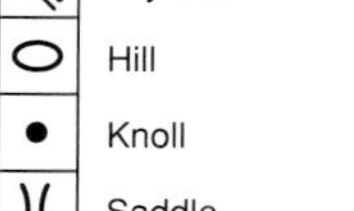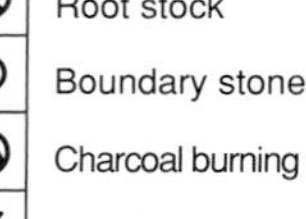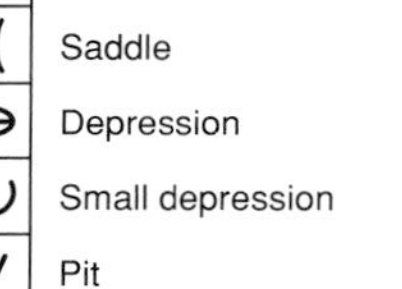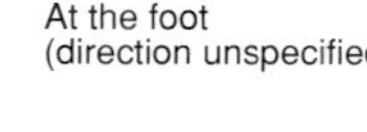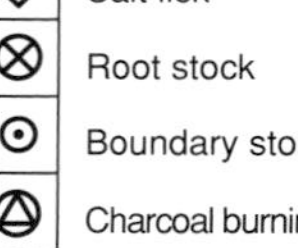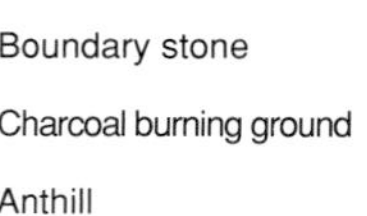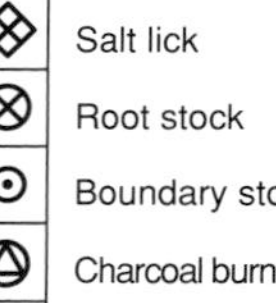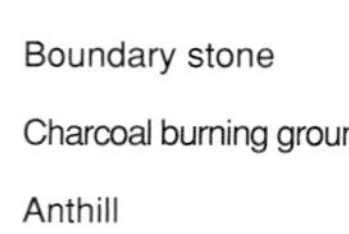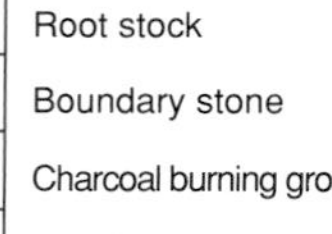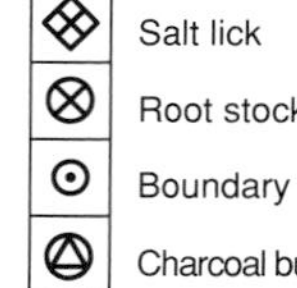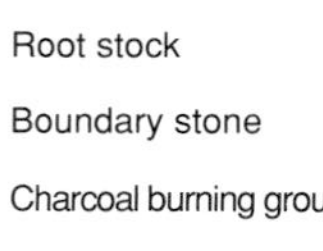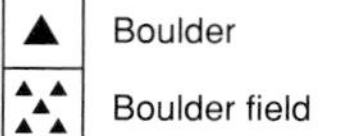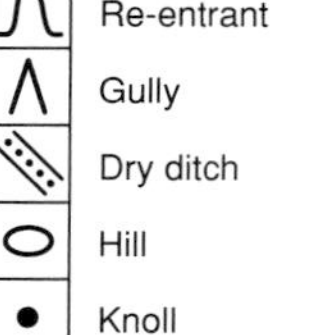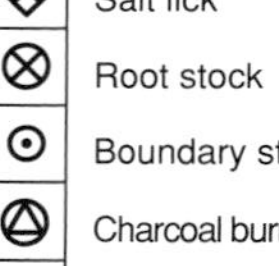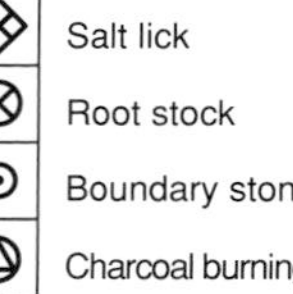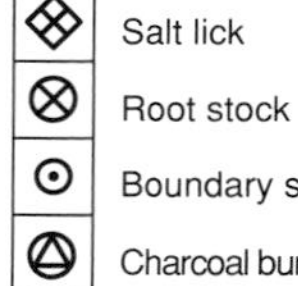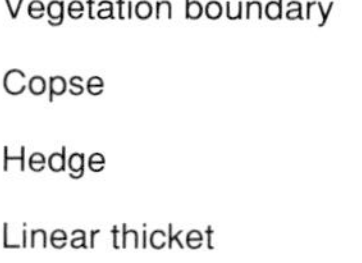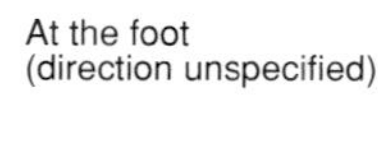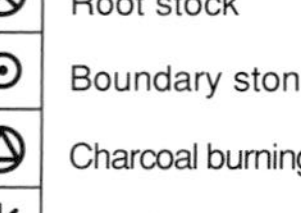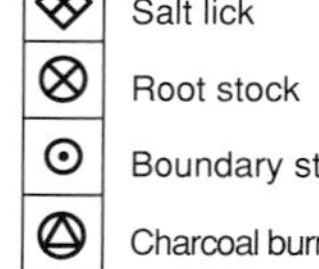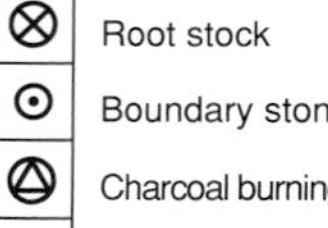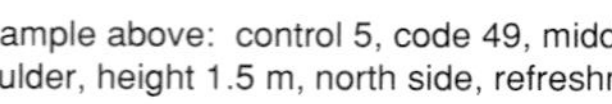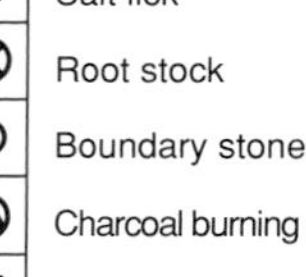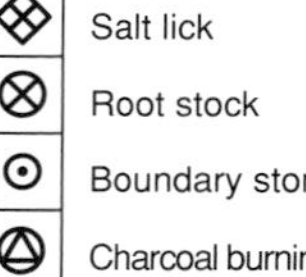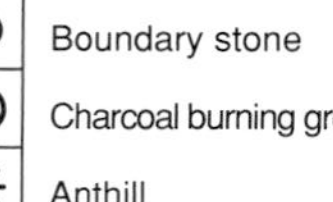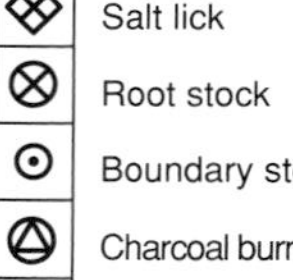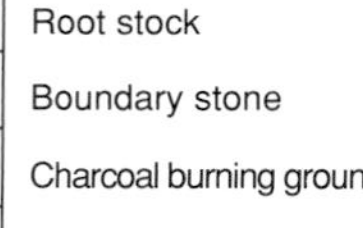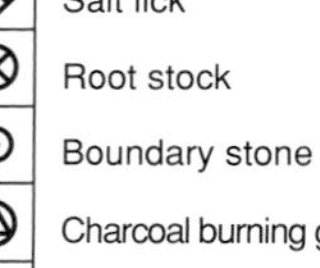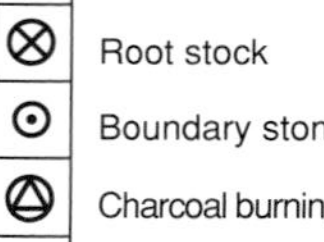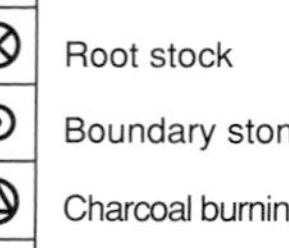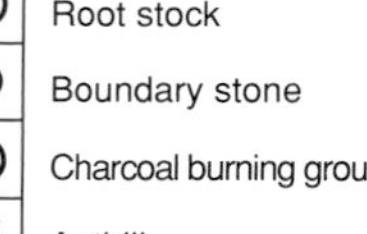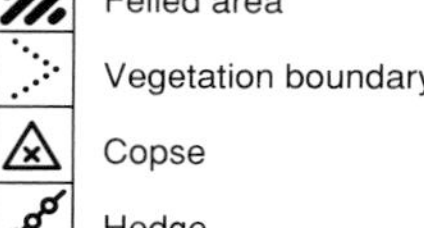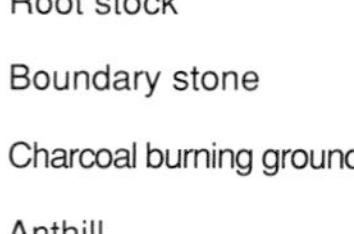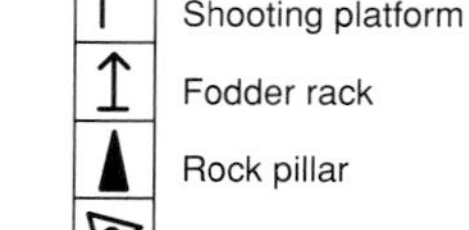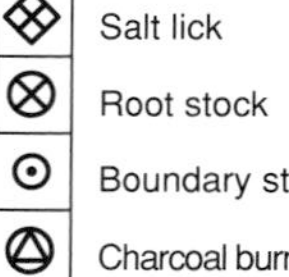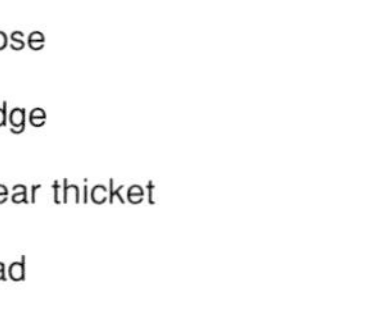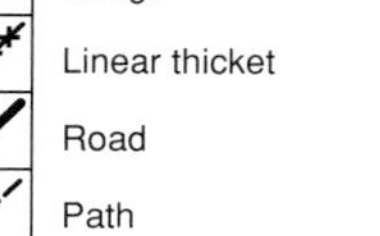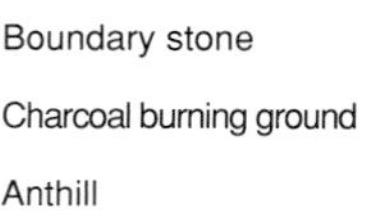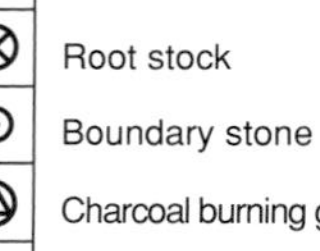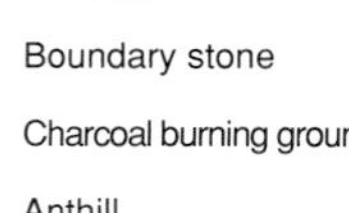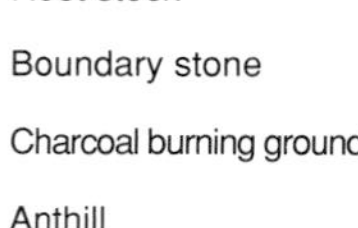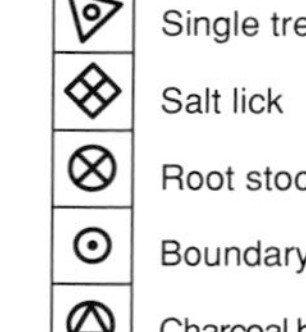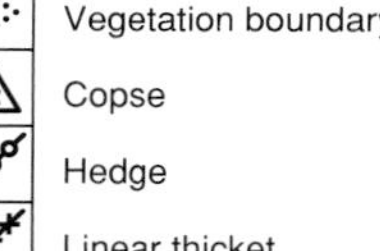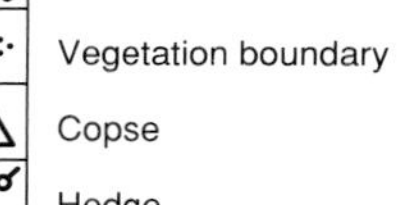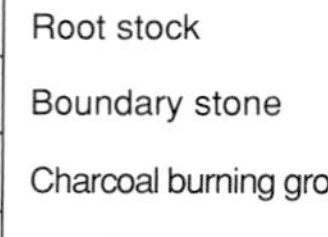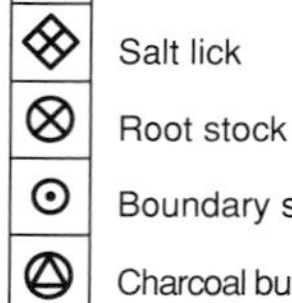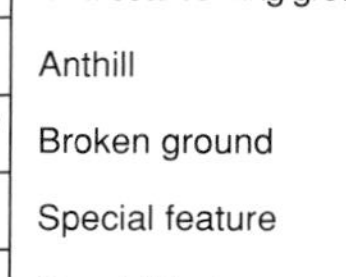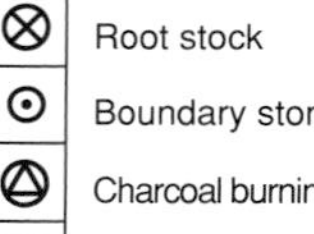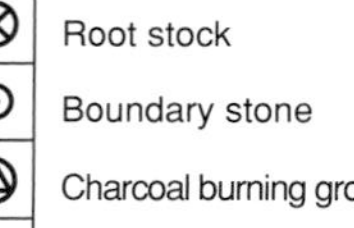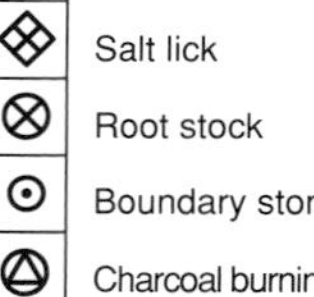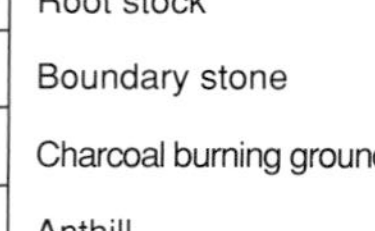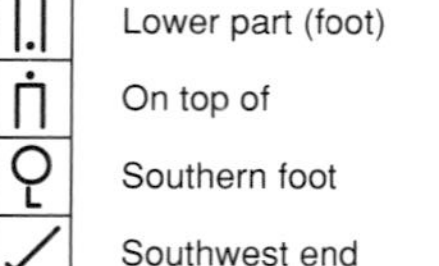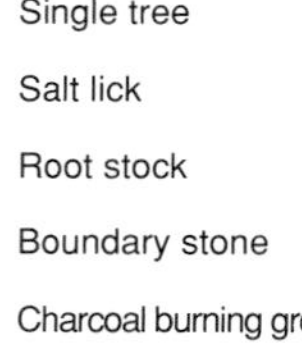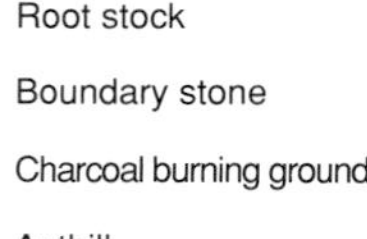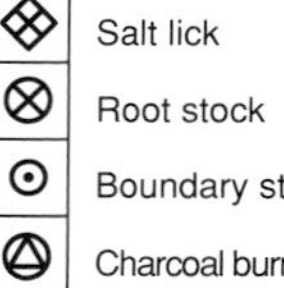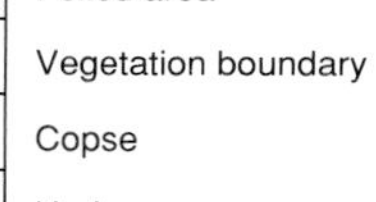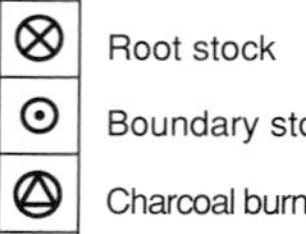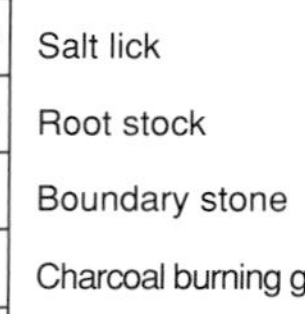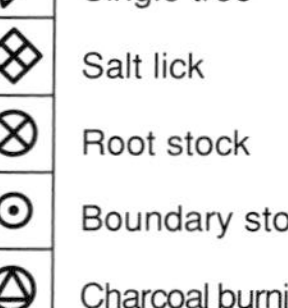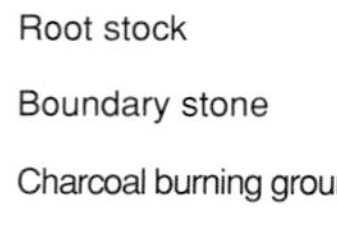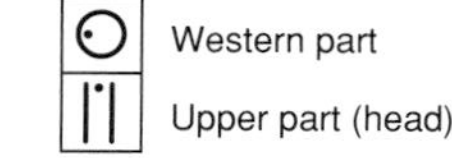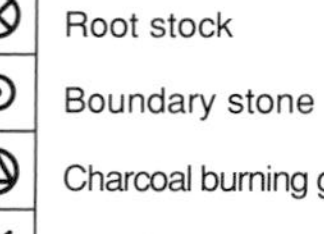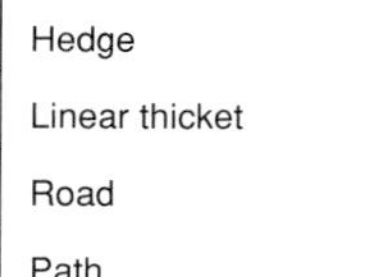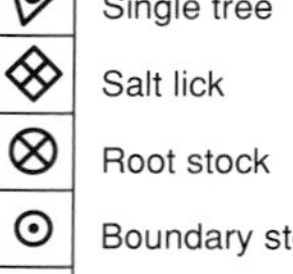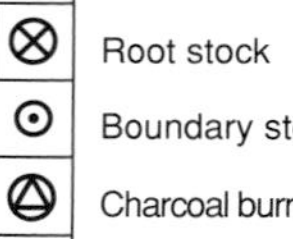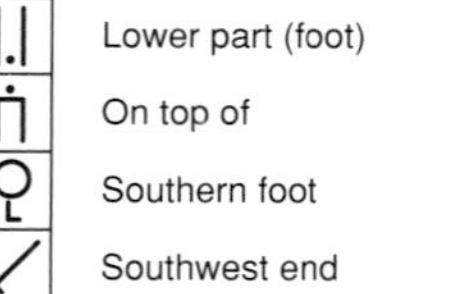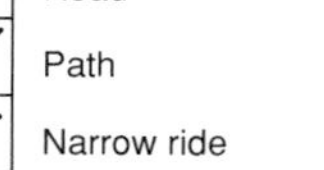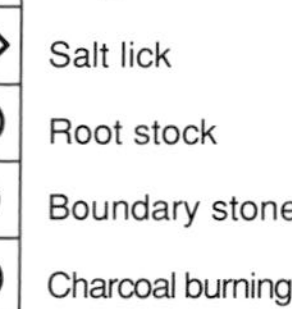

Appendix D

Control card for photocopying

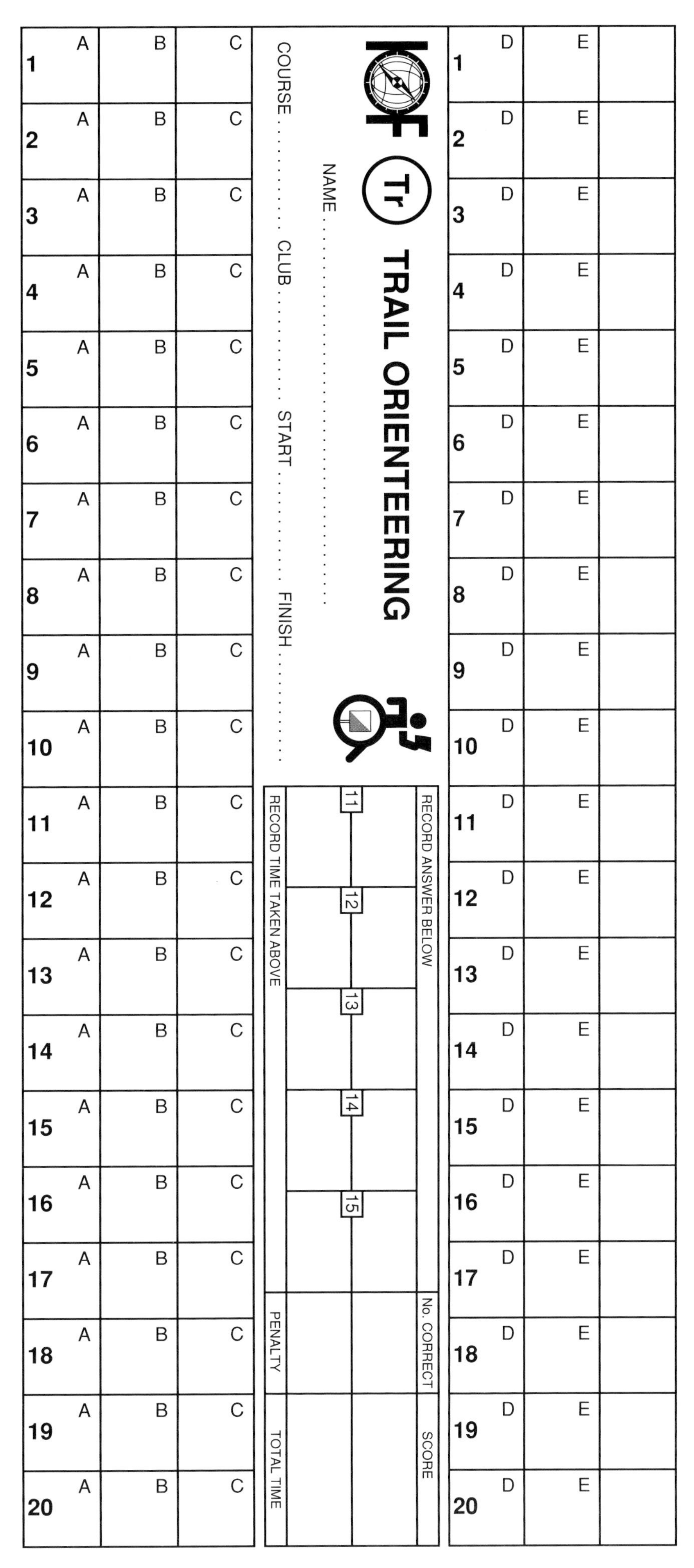

TRAIL ORIENTEERING

NAME ....

COURSE .... CLUB .... START .... FINISH ....

1	A	B	C	D	E	
2	A	B	C	D	E	
3	A	B	C	D	E	
4	A	B	C	D	E	
5	A	B	C	D	E	
6	A	B	C	D	E	
7	A	B	C	D	E	
8	A	B	C	D	E	
9	A	B	C	D	E	
10	A	B	C	D	E	
11	A	B	C	D	E	
12	A	B	C	D	E	
13	A	B	C	D	E	
14	A	B	C	D	E	
15	A	B	C	D	E	
16	A	B	C	D	E	
17	A	B	C	D	E	
18	A	B	C	D	E	
19	A	B	C	D	E	
20	A	B	C	D	E	

RECORD ANSWER BELOW

11	12	13	14	15

RECORD TIME TAKEN ABOVE

No. CORRECT		PENALTY
SCORE		TOTAL TIME

Appendix E

We have reproduced here an example of one club's initial experience with providing a Trail O course.

A. publicity sheet
B. map
C. control descriptions and basic instructions for the competition.

NORWICH ORIENTEERING CLUB

Even the simplest of orienteering courses usually involves the use of control points which even when close to a footpath are quite impossible for someone in a wheelchair to approach. TRAIL-O was developed in Scandinavia to allow people confined to wheelchairs to take part in orienteering, providing exercises in map reading and interpretation of the terrain. The general idea is that courses consist of control points which may be some distance from footpaths but are marked by several 'markers'. The problem is to identify the correctly placed 'marker'. Even with path networks it is possible to introduce the idea of 'route choice' - to choose the most efficient route between control points. The only equipment needed is a biro although you may find useful a polybag (to protect the map in the wet!), a clipboard (we can usually provide one), and possibly a compass (hirable from the club O-shop).

Future Events:

Sunday 11 October — ***Holt Country Park & Holt Lowes***
Colour Coded event & Trail-O

From Norwich, at Holt bypass, take A148 (Cromer Rd); after .25 mile turn right (Hempstead); after further mile turn right (map ref TG 086383) to park as directed - disabled should ask marshal if they can park on Park car park. Registration 10-12; starts 1030-1230; courses close 1430; fees (including results) - £1.50 seniors, 50p juniors (under 21); toilets in Holt town and in main Country Park car park; dogs allowed.

Trail-O: Starts - any time between 1100 and 1230; fee - 50p

Sunday 15 November — ***Pretty Corner, Sheringham***
Colour Coded, NOR Junior Champs & Trail-O

Look for O signs at junction of A148 (Holt-Cromer road) and A1082 (Sheringham Road) - parking at TG 151411; details as for Holt event; toilets at N Norfolk Railway Station at lower end of A1082; dogs allowed.

Trail-O: Starts and fees as for Holt.

Sunday 6 December — ***Kelling Caravan Park & Bodham Wood***
Colour Coded event & Trail-O

2.5 miles from Holt at Bodham, turn N off A148 to Weybourne; after 1 mile, turn left into Caravan Park and follow O signs to parking; details as for Holt event; toilets on caravan site; sorry, no dogs!

Trail-O: Starts and fees as for Holt.

PLEASE COME AND ENJOY OUR COURSES.

Kelling Heath Caravan Park
Trail-O

Information and instructions

The map is an enlarged and modified version of the original (coloured) one.

Keep to footpaths and tracks.

Don't necessarily follow the red lines!

When necessary, use the scale at the bottom of this sheet to measure distance on the map. Scale - 4mm on the map represents 10m on the ground.

When you have found a 'control' feature, decide which of the markers is correctly placed and tick the appropriate box.

The first few are very easy but then begin to get more difficult.

N, S, E, W = north, south, east, west.

A 'firepoint' is a large metal tripod.

The feature described will be found at the exact Centre of the Red Circle.

Control Descriptions

1 Firepoint
2 W of track junction
3 Firepoint

4 Wet depression
5 Building - E corner
6 Centre of clearing

7 E side of track
8 S of firepoint
9 E side of track

10 Ditch
11 W corner of building
12 S side of track

13 N of pond
14 W of firepoint
15 N side track junction

100m to Finish

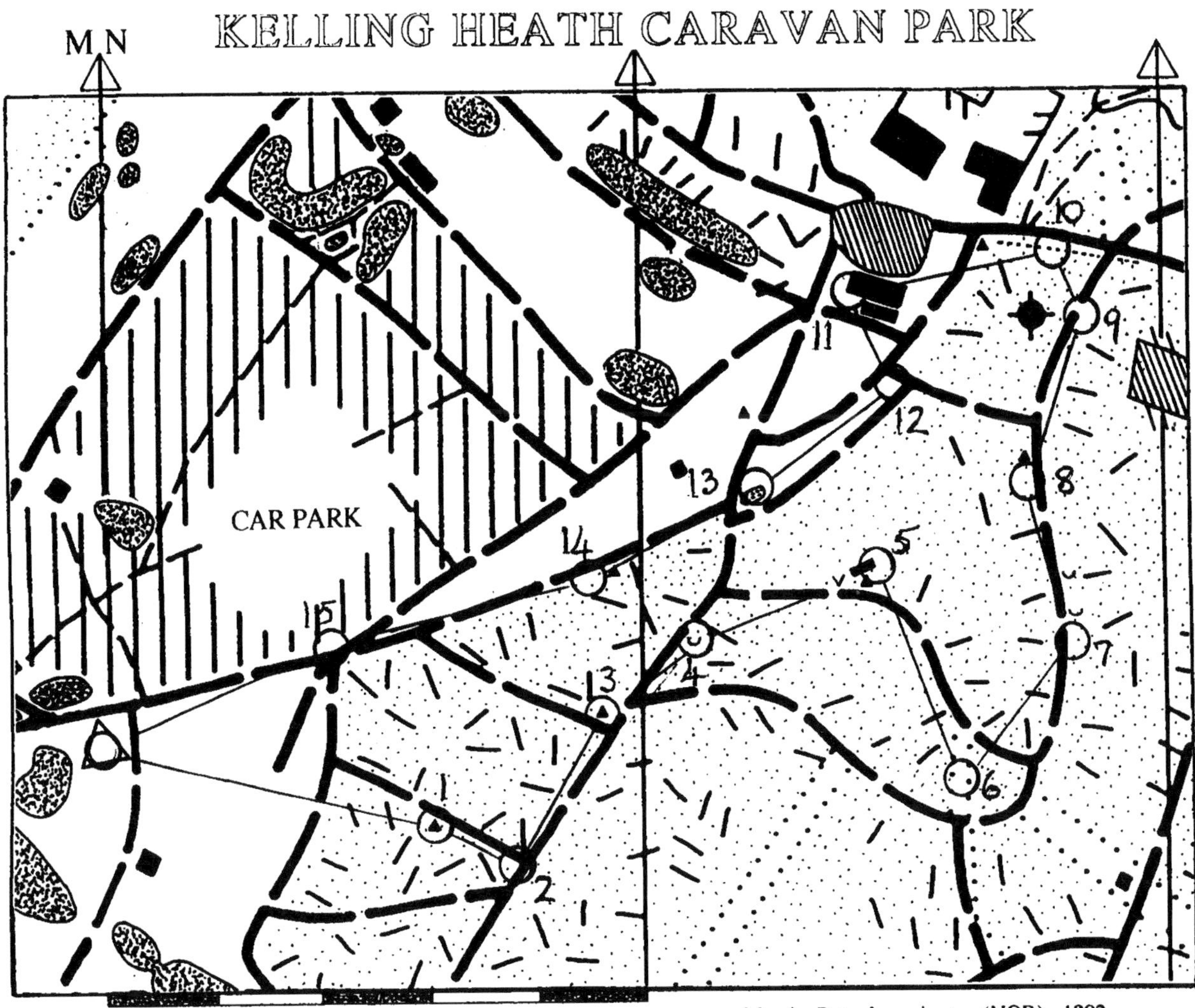

Map by Peter Leverington (NOR) - 1992
Modified for Trail-O by Mike George (NOR) - 1992

Appendix F Books and Sources

BOOKS

Orienteering in the National Curriculum Keystages 1 & 2
by Carol McNeill, Jim Martland & Peter Palmer (Harveys). ISBN 1 85137 0056

Orienteering in the National Curriculum Keystages 3 & 4
by Peter Palmer Carol McNeill (Harveys). ISBN 1 85137 0102.

Start Orienteering
by Carol McNeill and Tom Renfrew (Harveys).
A series of books of lesson plans for teachers.
Book 1 (6-8 year olds) ISBN 1 85137 0404.
Book 2 (8-9 year olds) ISBN 1 85137 0501
Book 3 (9-10 year olds) ISBN 1 85137 0331
Book 4 (10-12 year olds) ISBN 1 85137 0609
Book 6 Games & exercises ISBN 1 85137 0803

Teaching Orienteering
by Carol McNeill, Jean Ramsden and Tom Renfrew (Harveys).
Comprehensive manual with over 100 lesson plans. ISBN 1 85137 020X.

Mapmaking for Orienteers
by Robin Harvey (Harveys). ISBN 1 85137 0013.

Compass Sport: 37 Sandycoombe Rd, Twickenham, Middlesex TW1 2LR.
Magazine for orienteers, 8 issues per annum. Subscriptions: 25 The Hermitage, Elliot Hill, London, SE13 7EH. Tel. 081 852 1457.

SOURCES

Harveys: 12-16 Main Street, Doune, Perthshire, FK16 6BJ. Tel: 0786 841202. Fax: 0786 841098.
• Largest supplier of teaching resources, materials, books, videos and other audio-visual aids: equipment for organising orienteering.
• Mapmaking service, including map printing.
• Free catalogue available

Ultrasport: The Square, Newport, Salop, TF10 7AG. Tel: 0952 813918
Orienteering clothing, equipment and shoes. Ultrasport offers discounts for club and school group orders.

Silva UK Ltd: Unit 10 Sky Business Park, Eversley Way, Egham, Surrey, TW10 8RF. Tel: 0784 471721
Silva offer a range of orienteering equipment and kit, as well as the world renowned Silva compasses. Discounts are available for club and school group orders.

British Orienteering Federation, Riversdale, Dale Road North, Darley Dale, Matlock, Derbyshire, DE4 2JB. Tel: 0629 734042 (24 hour answering service). Fax: 0629 733769
BOF has introductory packs for individuals, clubs and schools, information on membership, permanent courses, coaching awards, schools schemes and fixtures. A limited number of videos are available on loan. A quarterly BOF News is sent to all members and affiliated organisations.